Sensationally

SUGAR FREE

**DELICIOUS SUGAR-FREE RECIPES FOR
HEALTHIER EATING EVERY DAY**

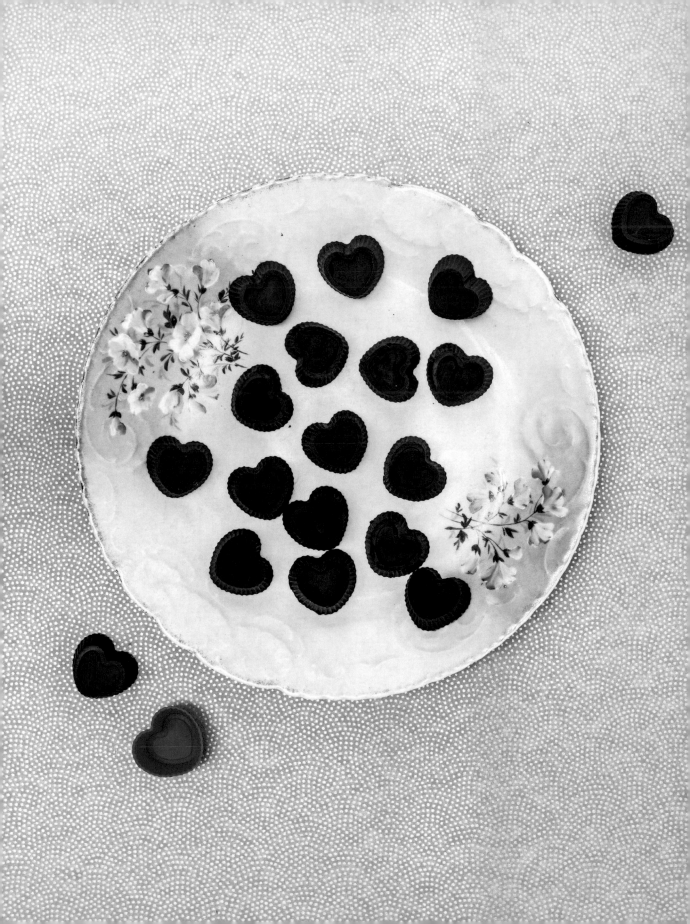

Sensationally SUGAR FREE

DELICIOUS SUGAR-FREE RECIPES FOR HEALTHIER EATING EVERY DAY

hamlyn

SUSANNA BOOTH

Contents

Introduction

You may wonder why a book of no added sugar recipes is full of sweet foods. Obviously, the way to avoid most sugar is simply never to eat anything sweet. However, eating is so much more than mere refueling. It is bound up with social convention, our emotions, and the habits we have developed over time.

I love sweet things. Whether it's a little something to finish off a meal, a midmorning snack, or a full-on overblown dessert for special occasions, I feel life would be incredibly diminished if I could eat only savory foods for the rest of it. But I also know that too much sweet food is bad for my health—dental and otherwise. Unless we are clawing our way across Antarctica in a blizzard, our daily nutritional needs for sugar are small.

The key is balance: some sweetness, but not too much; a good variety of foods; plenty of fiber; lots of vitamins; small portions. We all know it, but it's often easier said than done.

It is in this spirit that I have developed this book. Whatever your reasons for wanting to cut back on sugar, this collection of recipes can help. They combine the natural sweetness of fruits and vegetables with whole grains, nuts, and seeds to offer healthier alternatives to many of our favorite sugary dishes and treats.

Some of the cakes, ice creams, and desserts may be less sweet than those you've grown used to because it has become the norm for foods to contain high levels of sugar. But I believe that if you want to move away from a reliance on sugar, an important step is to become accustomed to things being a little less sweet. You'll find that quite quickly you won't notice a difference and may even experience a heightened sense of taste.

You'll soon see how easy and rewarding it is to go sugar free—no junk, just a sweeter way to live.

Susanna Booth

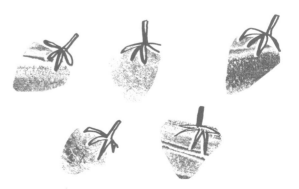

The Role of Sugar in the Diet

WHAT IS SUGAR?

Table sugar, granulated sugar, raw brown sugar, soft brown sugar… these familiar forms of sugar are all a substance known scientifically as sucrose. Sucrose is extracted from the juice of sugar cane or sugar beet and then processed and purified. The degree of refining affects the color and size of the crystals, but they are basically all the same product. Molasses and blackstrap molasses are by-products of sugar processing that still contain a high level of sucrose. All sugars have four calories per gram.

Sugar is a naturally derived product—the problem with it is that any vitamins, minerals, or fiber that were present in the original plant have been removed. This is why it is thought of as "empty calories"—it offers us energy, but nothing else that the body can use. This may be useful occasionally, but most of the time it's just not necessary, and can even be harmful.

Chemically speaking, "sugar" describes a group of related molecules. They are made up of carbon, hydrogen, and oxygen atoms, which is why they are also part of a larger group called carbohydrates. Sucrose is in fact made up of two simpler sugars—fructose and glucose—joined together, a bit like when you link two paperclips. Combinations of glucose or fructose molecules create many common carbohydrates, including fructo-oligosaccharides, maltose, maltodextrin, starch, and cellulose (fiber).

Glucose (also known as dextrose)

Glucose is found in a variety of foods: as well as fruit, it also occurs in low levels in grains, beans and vegetables. It is also added to food; it's a major component of glucose syrup.

Our cells rely on glucose to work—it's literally the fuel we need to survive. One of the main goals of our digestive system is to ensure glucose gets into our blood in order to be carried around the body to the cells.

Ideally, our bodies would like a steady trickle of glucose rather than a massive dose all at once. The extent to which foods raise the level of glucose in our bloodstream after eating gives us the "Glycemic Index" rating, more commonly known as GI. Pure glucose is rated 100, with other foods ranked in descending order. Unless we have been exercising strenuously, it's best to opt for foods with GI ratings of 65 and below, or combine a high-GI food (such as white bread with a GI of 70) with foods that either don't contain sugars or very low amounts (for example, foods that aren't carbohydrates, like eggs, meat, green vegetables, cheese, or cream).

Too much glucose can cause health problems, as highlighted on page 8.

Fructose (also known as laevulose)

Fructose is sometimes called "fruit sugar" because it is found in nearly all fruits. It tastes much sweeter than sucrose. After eating, it's transported to the liver, where much of it is converted to glucose. This means that its GI rating is low because the process is fairly slow.

Our ancestors would probably never have consumed more fructose in a day than that which was in the fruit/honey they ate, but these days it's possible to consume considerably more. This has been linked to a variety of health problems—see page 8 for more on this.

Problems caused by sugar

When glucose is produced during digestion, it enters the bloodstream and a hormone called insulin is released. Insulin helps certain cells store some of the glucose in a different form, called glycogen. The result is that the blood glucose levels fall to normal. If the levels drop below normal, glycogen is turned back into glucose. When the brain detects higher glucose levels, it stops hunger signals, which is why a steady intake of glucose (such as that created when complex carbohydrates are digested) helps to keep you feeling full for longer.

On a day-to-day level, eating too much sugary food in one go will result in a sudden large increase in blood glucose levels, only for them to drop very quickly. This could contribute to mood swings and tiredness, and can also make you feel very hungry again relatively quickly, which could lead to excess calorie consumption.

Excessive glucose

As described above, insulin is used to control the levels of glucose in the blood, with the excess being stored as glycogen. However, the body can only store a certain amount of glucose in this way, and any beyond that limit is converted to fat. A large excess can therefore lead to obesity.

Diabetes is the name given to a disease where insulin is either not produced at all, not produced in high enough concentrations or is faulty. This means that the level of glucose in the blood stays high. Left untreated, it can cause severe health complications.

Excessive fructose

Fructose, as mentioned before, is converted into glucose in the liver. However, the body is not able to absorb large amounts, so some of it is left over to be devoured by our gut bacteria instead. The bacteria release gas, which can lead to bloating and diarrhea. Some people have difficulty absorbing even small amounts of fructose, a condition known as fructose malabsorption.

Processing high levels of fructose also produces uric acid, which can result in gout, and has been linked to a higher risk of obesity and high blood pressure.

Sugar and teeth

Inside our mouths lives a colony of bacteria. These bacteria like sticking themselves to our teeth using a sort of starchy glue, which is also their food—we call this plaque. The bacteria make this glue by digesting carbohydrates found in our mouths, especially sugars like glucose, fructose, sucrose, and maltose. As they digest the sugar, an acid is produced. It is this acid that damages our tooth enamel and leads to decay.

These bacteria have always lived with us, but examination of the skulls of our ancestors from a thousand or so years ago often shows little tooth decay despite the lack of toothbrushes, toothpaste, etc. It seems that a combination of tough, fibrous breads, vegetables, and meat (lots of chewing) and limited sweet foods helped to keep the levels of plaque in check. In the UK, the widespread increase in tooth decay dates only from about 1600 onward—the time when large amounts of refined sugar became freely available.

Modern dental advice suggests brushing before breakfast, eating sweet foods only as part of a meal, avoiding "grazing" on sweet/starchy foods, drinking plenty of water (which rinses away sugars and acids), and brushing again before bed. Eating hard cheese or peanuts after a meal will help to make the mouth less acidic as well.

SUGAR ALTERNATIVES

There is no magic alternative to sugar—all have pros and cons. Some are naturally derived, such as sugar alcohols (maltitol, xylitol, and others) and stevia, though humans have never before been able to eat them to excess, while others are manmade, as in the artificial sweeteners, the long-term effects of which are still not fully known. Other options like honey, maple syrup, or fruit and vegetables still contain sucrose, glucose, and fructose, so in that respect they are not much different to table sugar.

Of all of them, using whole fruit and vegetables as sweeteners seems to me the most preferable because, not only are they "real foods," but there are also many added benefits. This is why I have based most of the recipes around fruit and vegetables. Fruit and vegetables, whether fresh or dried, almost all contain some level of sugar, be it sucrose, glucose, fructose, or all three. Some fruits—especially dried fruits like dates or raisins—can be considered high-sugar foods and you need to watch how much you eat. However, they offer many benefits, such as fiber, vitamins, and minerals. Large amounts of fiber help you to feel full, which may support portion control.

Where a little extra sweetness is required, I have used small quantities of stevia because it is naturally derived and does not cause tooth decay, but substitute it with a different sweetener if you prefer.

What is stevia?

Stevia rebaudiana is a plant with white flowers found in Brazil and Paraguay. Its leaves contain a cocktail of related chemicals called steviol glycosides (including steviosides and rebaudiosides), which have a sweetness over 200 times stronger than sucrose. It also has a slightly bitter aftertaste, which can be unpleasant. Stevia extracts are poorly metabolized, passing through the stomach and small intestine intact.

Bacteria in the large intestine then break the molecules down.

The stevia you can buy usually involves a refined extract of the leaf, blended with another sugar substitute to bulk it out and improve the flavor. Though sweetening agents in stevia leaves have no GI, no calories, and don't cause tooth decay, the bulking product may do, so check the label carefully.

Stevia extracts have been in use as a sweetener in Japan and other Asian countries for decades. In the European Union, stevia-based sweeteners were approved in 2011. Currently, the Food and Drug Administration (FDA) in the USA has not approved the whole leaf or crude extracts for use in food—only sweeteners using rebaudioside A have been accepted as GRAS (Generally Recognized As Safe). For more information, see www.fda.gov. Also, see page 187 for more about my use of stevia.

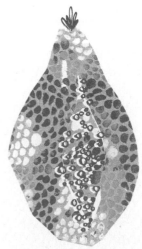

Simple Steps to Sugar-Free Eating

LIVING WITHOUT SUGAR

Despite the popularity of "paleo" diets that avoid grains, these kinds of complex carbohydrates have been the staple food of humans for thousands of years. For instance, the Romans, Ancient Greeks, and Ancient Egyptians all ate wheat-based bread every day and the Ancient Chinese ate rice, while early South American peoples such as the Olmec ate corn. Whole grains are a great energy source and they also make us feel full.

What wasn't eaten in bulk throughout the year in ancient times was masses of sugary foods made of simple carbohydrates—be it cakes and cookies or even honey or fruit.

In excess, such foods are bad news for our bodies and our teeth. Indeed, some experts believe that high-sugar diets are the biggest health problem facing mankind today.

The World Heath Organization's current guidelines recommend no more than 2 oz (10 teaspoons) of added sugar (including that from honey, maple syrup, juice, and fruit concentrates but not whole fruit and vegetables) per adult per day—you could reach this amount after just a bowl of cereal and a glass of orange juice. The WHO suggests that lowering that figure to a mere 1 oz (5 teaspoons) would be even more beneficial. It makes sense to choose your sweet foods carefully.

TOP TIPS FOR MINIMIZING SUGAR INTAKE

- **Avoid sweet drinks.** A can of full sugar cola contains 30–40 g (around 6–8 teaspoons) of sugar, so this is a really easy place to start cutting back. Incredibly, a 1¼ cup serving of fruit juice can often contain similar amounts—or even more! This is because it will be the juice of many fruits. Instead of drinking apple juice, for instance, eat an apple. It will taste just as sweet, but your total sugar consumption will be much lower and you'll have the benefit of the fiber as well.
- **Avoid sweetened sauces or dressings.** Salad dressings, ketchup, sweet chili sauce, pickles, and even mustard can all contain sugar—these "hidden" sugars can soon add up. Try vinaigrette or real mayonnaise as an alternative.
- **Be careful about breakfast choices.** Many cereals contain high levels of sugar. Instead opt for foods like oatmeal, eggs, plain yogurt, or whole-wheat bread with cheese.
- **Minimize alcohol consumption.** Alcohol is created when yeasts break down sugar. If that process isn't completed, sugar can remain, as in the case of sweet white wines, cider, or beer. Spirits are a better choice, sugarwise; use an unsweetened mixer like soda water.
- **Go raw and fresh where you can.** Many fruits taste sweeter raw than cooked, and food at room temperature will taste sweeter than the same food when frozen.
- **Sprinkle with powdered sweetener.** If you like adding sweetener to fruit or cereal, for example, a light dusting of a powdered product can often be just as effective tastewise as a heavy sprinkling of granulated sugar or a drizzling of syrup.

COOKING WITHOUT SUGAR

As well as acting as a sweetener, sugar also plays a role in the texture of foods. For instance, it is sugar's ability to melt into a hard glasslike caramel that helps give the strength to a finished meringue or the "snap" in certain kinds of cookie. The fudgy texture of sugar heated with butter is what makes chewy cookies or brownies so moreish. And the presence of sugar is also an integral part of smooth ice creams and sorbets because it acts like antifreeze, preventing the growth of large ice crystals.

This means that successful cooking without sugar is not always just a matter of leaving it out or replacing it with another kind of sweetener because many of the alternatives don't behave in the same way. Careful thought is often required in order to achieve good results. I've tried to create healthy versions of favorite recipes—using whole foods where possible—that emulate the textures normally associated with those dishes. For instance, I use butternut squash to make my brownies chewy (see page 130), and for my squidgy cookies I use banana (see page 33). I've even managed to create silky ice creams with the help of agar powder, whose large molecular structure helps keep ice crystals to a minimum (see page 186).

TOP TIPS FOR CREATING SUGAR-FREE RECIPES

- **Mix stevia powder with liquid before use.** Stevia is so supersweet that its granules can taste unpleasant, while its bitter flavors can be noticeable when used in large amounts. I've found I get the best results when I dissolve it in liquid before adding it to my recipe. Add it gradually —it's surprising how little you need.
- **Stick to "nuggets" of sweetness.** Sometimes this is all that's necessary to make something tasty. If your cake has small pieces of sweet foods, such as raisins, chopped apricots, and pieces of fruit, you can reduce the sweetness of the cake batter without really noticing.
- **Try to exploit naturally sweet foods.** Rice milk, evaporated milk, cashew nuts, fresh fruit, dried fruit, and vegetables like carrots are among the foods that are naturally sweet. If you add them to recipes you can cut back on added sweeteners.
- **Opt for the freshest, best-quality apple juice or orange juice**. Cloudy apple juices and the type of orange juice that still has bits both have more micronutrients than the juices that have been filtered and concentrated.
- **Be creative with toppings.** One of the drawbacks of going sugar free is that most cake toppings (be it confectioners' sugar, frosting, or sugar sprinkles) involve sugar in some form. Try decorating cakes with whipped cream, cream cheese, whole nuts, or fresh or dried fruit instead. Wafer shapes, cocoa, edible glitter, and edible flowers are great for achieving that wow factor.
- **Use whole foods where possible.** This can include seeds, whole nuts, whole grains, whole fruit and vegetables (try to keep the skin on if you can). You might only include a small amount, but that doesn't matter—some is always better than none.
- **Eat smart.** Using sugar alternatives is not a license to eat large amounts of sweet foods. Keeping portion sizes small and infrequent means that you can still enjoy cakes and desserts, but overall sugar consumption will be lower.

Recipe Finder

RECIPE FINDER

EVERYDAY SNACKS

	Page	Dairy-free	Gluten-free	Contains no eggs	Contains no nuts	Vegetarian	Vegan
Cream Cheese & Apple Twists	104	○	○	○	●	●	○
Peanut Snack Bars	106	●	○	○	○	●	●
Chocolate & Rye Energy Bars	108	●	○	●	○	●	●
Raw Gingerbread	109	●	○	●	○	●	●
Banana Bread	111	○	○	○	●	●	○
Cardamom Waffles with Berries	112	○	○	○	●	●	○
Swedish Cherry Buns	114	○	○	○	●	●	○
Fruit Braid	117	○	○	●	●	●	○
Apple Oatmeal	118	○	○	●	●	●	●
Mango & Cranberry Muesli	119	●	○	●	●	●	●
Poppy Seed Grissini	120	○	○	●	●	●	○
Smoked Cheese & Apple Scones	121	○	○	○	●	●	○
Spiced Trail Mix	123	●	●	●	○	●	●
Pumpkin Pops	123	●	○	●	●	●	●

FOR CHILDREN

	Page	Dairy-free	Gluten-free	Contains no eggs	Contains no nuts	Vegetarian	Vegan
Cheesy Breadsticks	126	○	○	●	●	●	●
Tomato & Herb Spirals	129	○	○	●	●	●	●
Chocolate Brownies	130	○	○	○	●	●	○
Magic Pancakes	133	○	○	○	●	●	○
Apple Freezer Flapjacks	134	○	○	●	●	●	○
Chocolate Refrigerator Cake	135	○	○	●	●	●	○
Sticky Doughnut Buns	136	○	○	○	●	●	○
Ginger Stars	138	○	○	●	●	●	○
Crispy Cakes	139	○	●	●	●	●	○
Apple & Blackberry Parcels	141	○	○	●	○	●	○
Pineapple Fritters	142	○	○	○	●	●	○
Stripy Snow Cones	145	●	●	●	●	●	●

TREATS & PARTY FOOD

	Page	Dairy-free	Gluten-free	Contains no eggs	Contains no nuts	Vegetarian	Vegan
Glittering Chocolate Truffles	148	○	●	●	●	●	○
Apricot Hearts	151	○	●	●	○	●	○
Mini Chocolate Eclairs	152	○	○	○	●	●	○
Rocky Road	154	○	●	●	○	●	○
Macadamia Chews	155	○	●	●	○	●	○
Chocolate Fondue	157	○	●	●	●	●	○
Baklava	159	○	○	●	○	●	○
Mint Chocolate Crunch	160	○	●	●	●	●	○
Cinnamon Toasts	161	●	○	●	●	●	○
Toffee-Flavored Popcorn	162	○	●	●	●	●	○
Sweet Chile Bites	163	○	●	●	●	●	○
Butter-Fried Plantains with Smoky Dip	165	○	●	●	●	●	○

SAUCES, SPREADS & OTHER BASICS

	Page	Dairy-free	Gluten-free	Contains no eggs	Contains no nuts	Vegetarian	Vegan
Velvet Hot Chocolate	168	○	●	●	●	●	○
Low-Carb Dessert Dough	170	○	○	●	●	●	○
Whipped Cake Frosting	171	○	●	●	●	●	○
Vanilla Cream	172	○	●	●	●	●	○
Orange Dessert Sauce	173	○	●	●	●	●	○
Mango Coulis	174	●	●	●	●	●	●
Mixed Berry Compote	175	●	●	●	●	●	●
Orange & Apricot Curd	176	○	●	○	●	●	○
Strawberry Jam	178	●	●	●	●	●	●
Chocolate Hazelnut Spread	179	○	●	●	○	●	○
Quick Apple Pickle	180	●	●	●	●	●	●
Asian-Style Dipping Sauce	181	○	○	●	●	●	●
Tomato Ketchup	182	●	●	●	●	●	●
Avocado Mayonnaise	184	●	●	○	●	●	○
Vinaigrette Dressing	185	●	●	●	○	●	●

Please note this is a guideline only; all ingredients should be checked for suitability before use.

Muffins, Cupcakes & Cookies

Airy chocolate muffins oozing little nuggets of melted chocolate are one of the finest sights to emerge from an oven. Even better is the fact that muffins benefit from a laid-back approach, so this is seriously easy baking that anyone can master.

Double Chocolate Muffins

MAKES 12

1¾ cups all-purpose flour
3 tablespoons unsweetened cocoa
3 teaspoons baking powder
1 cup rice milk
½ cup sunflower oil
3 eggs, beaten
2 teaspoons unsweetened vanilla
  extract
2 teaspoons stevia powder
  (see page 187)
5 oz no-added-sugar milk chocolate,
  chopped into chunks

Preheat the oven to 350°F. Line a 12-section muffin pan with paper muffin liners.

Mix the flour, cocoa, and baking powder together in a bowl. Stir the rice milk, oil, eggs, vanilla extract, and stevia powder together in a small bowl.

Pour the liquid mixture into the bowl and give a quick stir. It doesn't matter if there are still a few lumps—undermixing is better than stirring for too long, which can lead to a chewy, rather than airy, texture. Stir in the chocolate chunks.

You'll now have a sloppy brown batter. Divide the muffin batter evenly between the muffin liners.

Bake the muffins for 15–20 minutes until risen and springy to the touch, and an inserted toothpick comes out clean. Let them cool on a wire rack before serving. These muffins are lovely warm, but even better the following day. They also freeze well.

Almonds are one of nature's superfoods and combining them with cherries is a surefire way to get a tasty result. Almond milk gives an extra nutrient hit and also makes these muffins a dairy-free treat.

Cherry & Almond Muffins

MAKES 12

1⅔ cups ground almonds
1¼ cups all-purpose flour
3 teaspoons baking powder
generous ¾ cup unsweetened
   almond milk
⅓ cup sunflower oil
3 eggs, beaten
2 tablespoons stevia powder
   (see page 187)
1½ teaspoons unsweetened almond
   extract
10 oz fresh cherries, pitted and
   halved
2 tablespoons slivered almonds

Preheat the oven to 400°F. Line a 12-section muffin pan with paper muffin liners.

Mix the ground almonds, flour, and baking powder together in a bowl. Stir the almond milk, oil, eggs, stevia powder, and almond extract together in a small bowl.

Pour the liquid mixture into the dry ingredients and give everything a quick stir until combined. Stir in the cherry halves.

Divide the muffin batter evenly between the muffin liners. Sprinkle a few of the slivered almonds on top of each one.

Bake the muffins for 15–20 minutes until risen and golden brown, and an inserted toothpick comes out clean. Let them cool on a wire rack. Store the muffins in the refrigerator and eat within a couple of days.

Forget sugary cereals and try these awesome muffins for breakfast instead. Filling and nutritious, the combination of superfoods and protein will give your morning just the boost it needs. I like to make a batch and pop them in the freezer, defrosting them in the microwave as needed so that I always have some to hand.

Seeded Breakfast Muffins

MAKES 12

1¾ cups all-purpose flour
generous ¾ cup drained canned corn kernels
5 oz soft pitted prunes
⅓ cup sunflower seeds
⅓ cup finely grated carrot
1 cup unsweetened almond milk
½ cup sunflower oil
3 eggs
3 teaspoons unsweetened vanilla extract
3 teaspoons baking powder
1 teaspoon ground cinnamon
2 tablespoons pumpkin seeds

Preheat the oven to 350°F. Line a 12-section muffin pan with paper muffin liners.

Place all the ingredients except the pumpkin seeds in a food processor and blend for 10–15 seconds until everything is combined.

Pour the muffin batter into the muffin liners, ensuring you have distributed it evenly. Sprinkle the pumpkin seeds on the top of each muffin.

Bake the muffins for 25 minutes until risen and golden brown, and an inserted toothpick comes out clean. Let them cool in the pan. These are great either warm or cold, perhaps spread with a little butter. Store the muffins in the refrigerator and eat within a couple of days.

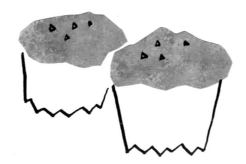

Don't knock a savory muffin until you've tried one, and few are as mouthwatering as these, with their light sage flavor and crowning dollop of sour cream and bacon.

Sage Muffins with Sour Cream & Bacon

MAKES 8

1 teaspoon sunflower oil

4 unsmoked lean bacon slices, finely chopped

½ cup sour cream

2 oz cheddar cheese or other hard cheese

1¼ cups all-purpose flour

1 tablespoon finely chopped sage

2 teaspoons baking powder

⅓ cup sunflower oil

¾ cup milk

2 eggs

Preheat the oven to 400°F. Line 8 sections of a 12-section muffin pan with paper muffin liners.

Heat the oil in a skillet and fry the chopped bacon until crisp. Stir the bacon bits into the sour cream and set aside.

Coarsely shred the cheese into a bowl. Stir in the flour, sage, and baking powder.

Whisk the oil, milk, and eggs together in a separate bowl. Pour the eggy liquid into the flour mixture and give a good, brisk stir until everything is combined. You'll now have a sloppy batter.

Pour the muffin batter evenly into the muffin liners. Top each one with about a tablespoonful of the sour cream and bacon, dolloped into the center.

Bake the muffins for 15 minutes until risen and browned—the sour cream will have remained at the top of each muffin. Let the muffins cool on a wire rack before serving. These are best eaten on the day they are made.

Tip

A mezzaluna, consisting of a single or double curved blade with a handle at either end, makes chopping fresh herbs incredibly easy and quick.

Roquefort cheese might seem a strange addition to muffins, but it works really well without being overly cheesy. My two-year-old will happily eat these, yet there is no way he would ever eat Roquefort, walnuts or, to be honest, even pears by themselves. These are delicious hot or cold, but best enjoyed on the day they are made.

Roquefort & Pear Muffins

MAKES 12

4 small Williams pears, about 13 oz
   total weight
½ cup crumbled Roquefort cheese
   or other blue cheese
3 eggs
¾ cup sunflower oil
4 tablespoons milk
1½ teaspoons unsweetened vanilla
   extract
generous ¾ cup whole-wheat all-
   purpose flour
generous ¾ cup all-purpose flour
4 teaspoons baking powder
1 cup walnuts, chopped

Preheat the oven to 400°F. Line a 12-section muffin pan with paper muffin liners.

Remove the cores from the pears (leave the skin on). Chop one into small chunks about ½ inch in size and set aside. Place the remaining pears in a blender with the cheese, eggs, oil, milk, and vanilla extract and blend until smooth.

Transfer to a bowl and stir in both flours and the baking powder, then stir in the walnuts and reserved chopped pear.

Divide the muffin batter evenly between the muffin liners and bake for 20 minutes until risen and browned. Serve straightaway or let cool on a wire rack before serving.

I have a total weakness for hazelnut lattes, a habit that I try to keep to an absolute minimum for the sake of my teeth and general health! It was, however, the inspiration for these cupcakes—they provide the nutty–coffee flavors and frothy sweetness that I love, just without a load of sugar.

Hazelnut Cappuccino Cupcakes

MAKES 12

3 tablespoons stevia powder
   (see page 187)
2 tablespoons instant coffee
2 teaspoons balsamic vinegar
2 tablespoons boiling water
scant ½ cup whole-wheat all-
   purpose flour
scant ½ cup all-purpose flour
5 tablespoons unsalted butter,
   very soft, chopped
2 eggs, beaten
1 teaspoon baking soda
¼ cup whole hazelnuts, chopped

For the topping
1 cup whipping cream
1 teaspoon stevia powder
   (see page 187)
½ teaspoon unsweetened vanilla
   extract
unsweetened cocoa, for dusting

Preheat the oven to 350°F. Line a 12-section muffin pan with paper muffin liners.

Stir the stevia powder, instant coffee, balsamic vinegar, and measurement boiling water together in a small bowl until you have a thick, dark liquid—it doesn't matter if the stevia hasn't completely dissolved.

Place both flours, butter, eggs, and baking soda in a bowl. Add the coffee mixture and whisk everything together for a minute until fluffy and well combined. Fold in the nuts, then dollop a tablespoonful of the cupcake batter into each muffin liner.

Bake for 12–15 minutes until risen and browned, and an inserted toothpick comes out clean. Transfer to a wire rack and let cool completely.

To make the topping, whip the cream with the stevia powder and vanilla extract until it forms firm peaks. Place in a pastry bag fitted with a large star tip then pipe onto the cupcakes. Finish by sifting cocoa onto the top of each one. The finished cupcakes should be kept in the refrigerator until ready to serve and are best eaten the same day.

Variation

For a different slant on this recipe, smear a little of my Chocolate Hazelnut Spread (see page 179) on the top of each cupcake instead of the sweetened cream.

The delicate creamy sweetness of coconut is used to full effect as a topping for moist lemon sponge. Coconut milk varies: for best results, choose coconut milk with at least 18 percent fat, and avoid brands with added sodium metabisulfite, as it can have an unpleasant taste.

Lemon Coconut Cupcakes

MAKES 12

1 (14 oz) can coconut milk, chilled
3 tablespoons stevia powder
  (see page 187)
1¼ cups all-purpose flour
2 teaspoons baking powder
⅓ cup sunflower oil
2 eggs, beaten
grated rind of 1 unwaxed lemon
  and 2 tablespoons juice

For the topping
¼ cup dry unsweetened coconut
1 teaspoon stevia powder
  (see page 187)
½ cup whipping cream

Preheat the oven to 350°F. Line a 12-section muffin pan with paper muffin liners.

Open the can of coconut milk, then scoop out the thick coconut "cream" from the top of the can into a large bowl and set aside. Pour ½ cup of the remaining watery coconut milk into a separate large bowl. Stir in the stevia powder, then add the flour, baking powder, oil, eggs, and lemon rind and juice. Give everything a quick and thorough whisk and then divide the batter evenly between the muffin liners.

Bake the cupcakes for 20 minutes until risen and just browned, and an inserted toothpick comes out clean. Let cool completely on a wire rack.

To make the topping, gently toast the dry unsweetened coconut in a dry skillet for 2 minutes, stirring occasionally, until golden. Let cool completely.

Add the stevia powder to the reserved coconut "cream." Using an electric whisk, whip until it forms soft peaks—this may take up to 4 minutes. Whip the whipping cream until it forms firm peaks, then fold into the coconut cream. Use a tablespoon to swirl a dollop onto each of the cupcakes and sprinkle the tops of them with the toasted dry unsweetened coconut. These cakes will keep for a couple of days in the refrigerator.

Variation

For a completely dairy-free alternative, make the topping using only the thick coconut "cream" scooped from the can. Stir in 1 teaspoon stevia powder and a pinch of xanthan gum, then whisk until it forms firm peaks. Spread onto the cupcakes and sprinkle with dry unsweetend coconut.

These buttery, wafer-thin cookies are part Swedish pepparkaka and part delicate tuile. Their light and airy crispness makes them perfect served alongside coffee or as an accompaniment to ice cream. The apple and cinnamon flavor is just heavenly too.

Cinnamon Thins

MAKES 18

1 egg white
4 tablespoons unsweetened apple puree
2 teaspoons stevia powder (see page 187)
1 teaspoon ground cinnamon
¼ cup all-purpose flour
2 tablespoons unsalted butter, melted

Preheat the oven to 325°F. Line a couple of baking sheets with silicone parchment paper.

Whisk the egg white in a bowl until it forms a thick froth, then whisk in the apple puree, stevia powder, and cinnamon.

Stir the flour and melted butter together in a small bowl. Fold into the egg white mix until you have a pale brown, thick batter.

Dollop a heaping teaspoonful of the batter onto one of the baking sheets. Use the back of a tablespoon to smooth it out evenly into a circle about 3 inches in diameter and about 1/16 inch thick—use a cookie cutter as a guide if you want them perfectly round, or cut a circle out of a piece of card to make a template. Repeat until you have filled the baking sheets.

Bake the thins for about 30 minutes until they have darkened and look dry—start checking them after 20 minutes. Transfer them to a wire rack. They will still be soft while they are hot, but once they have cooled they should be completely hard and crisp. They will keep for about a week, stored in an airtight container.

These luscious and very grown-up sandwich cookies feature a frozen lime cheesecake filling encased within salted crackers. Try them as a modern twist on ice cream in a cone, or serve as a quick and easy party snack.

Salted Lime Sandwich Cookies

MAKES 6

grated rind of ½ unwaxed lime
    and 1½ tablespoons juice
1 tablespoon white rum
1 tablespoon stevia powder
    (see page 187)
2 tablespoons cream cheese
½ cup heavy cream
12 salted whole-wheat crackers

Stir together the lime rind and juice, rum, and stevia powder in a cup until the stevia has dissolved. Stir in the cream cheese until smooth.

Whip the cream in a small bowl (see Tip) until it forms firm peaks. Stir in the lime mixture. Sandwich a tablespoonful of the resulting rather sloppy cream between 2 crackers and press down lightly (the cream shouldn't ooze out from between the crackers). Repeat for the remaining crackers.

Place all the sandwich cookies on a tray or plate and then freeze them for 15 minutes until the filling has become firm. They are now ready to eat.

Tip

A quick way to whip cream without it spattering everywhere is to pour it into a small bowl or pitcher and to use an immersion blender. This can work too well, in that it becomes easy to overwhip the cream, so go easy.

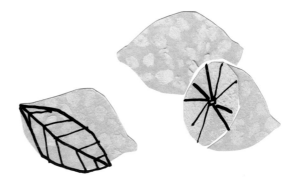

With just four ingredients, these cookies are simplicity itself, but none the worse for that. What makes them so irresistible is the way the chewy raisins burst through the oats, which have a lovely, almost buttery, crunch. Serve with a glass of milk for a perfect midmorning pick-me-up.

Oatmeal Raisin Cookies

MAKES 35

3½ cups jumbo rolled oats
1 cup raisins
⅓ cup sunflower oil,
    plus extra for oiling
¾ cup boiling water
all-purpose flour, for dusting

Preheat the oven to 300°F. Lightly oil a couple of baking sheets with a little sunflower oil.

Place the oats and half the raisins in a food processor. Pulse until you have a mixture with the texture of bread crumbs. Add the oil and measurement boiling water and continue to pulse until everything comes together as a soft dough. Stir in the remaining raisins, then let the dough sit and absorb the moisture for a couple of minutes.

Roll out the dough on a counter well dusted with flour to a thickness of ¼ inch. Use a 2½ inch round cookie cutter to cut out circles, rerolling the trimmings as necessary, until you have used up all the dough. Place the dough circles on the baking sheets.

Bake for 45 minutes until the cookies are golden brown, then switch the oven off and leave the cookies in the oven for another 20 minutes until they have become completely hard. Let cool completely on a wire rack and store in an airtight tin. They will keep for up to a week.

Variation

You can make a gluten-free version of these cookies by using gluten-free oats and dusting your counter with cornstarch when rolling out.

These are proper doughy cookies, with a crunchy crust and chewy center. However, unlike regular cookies, these are full of fiber and other goodness.

Date & Walnut Cookies

MAKES 12

1 banana, about 5 oz
3 oz pitted soft dried dates
3½ tablespoons whole-wheat all-purpose flour
2 tablespoons unsalted butter, cut into chunks, plus extra for greasing
¾ cup walnuts, chopped
4 tablespoons milk
pinch of salt

Preheat the oven to 350°F. Lightly grease a couple of baking sheets with a little butter.

Peel the banana and place in a food processor with the dates. Process for 4–5 seconds until the dates are in small pieces and the banana has become mashed, though your mixture should still have some texture (you don't want a puree).

Place the flour in a bowl, add the butter, and rub in with your fingertips until the mixture resembles bread crumbs. Add the date mixture, walnuts, milk, and salt and stir everything together.

Use a tablespoon to place the batter in 12 dollops on the baking sheets, spaced well apart. Use the back of the spoon to smear the dollops into rough circles about 3 inches in diameter and about ¼ inch thick (if you want neat circles, use a cookie cutter as a guide).

Bake the cookies for 20–25 minutes until the edges have become browned and hard, but the centers are still a little soft. Let cool on a wire rack and then store in an airtight container. They will keep for 2–3 days.

A combination of dried figs and whole almonds lends an attractive mosaiclike effect to these vanilla-flavored cookies. Try them alongside an espresso—they make a great alternative to sugary biscotti.

Almond & Fig Cookies

MAKES 25

generous ¾ cup all-purpose flour
½ cup ground almonds
5 tablespoons unsalted butter, chilled and cut into chunks, plus extra for greasing
1 egg, beaten
1 tablespoon stevia powder (see page 187)
1 teaspoon unsweetened vanilla extract
3¼ oz dried figs, stalks removed and finely chopped
¼ cup whole almonds, coarsely chopped

Place the flour, ground almonds, and butter in a food processor and pulse until you have a mixture with the texture of coffee grounds.

Stir the egg, stevia powder, and vanilla extract together in a small bowl. Pour the mixture into the food processor and then pulse until all the ingredients come together as a dough.

Remove the dough from the food processor and knead in the figs and almonds until well combined. Shape the dough into a rectangular block about 5 x 3¼ inches, and about 1½ inches thick. Place it in the freezer for an hour until it has become firm.

Preheat the oven to 350°F. Lightly grease a baking sheet with a little butter.

Remove the dough block from the freezer. Using a sharp knife, carefully cut the block into slices no more than ¼ inch thick. You may need to use a slight sawing action in order to cut neatly through the figs.

Place the cookies on the baking sheet and bake for 15–20 minutes until lightly browned and hardened. Let cool on a wire rack, then store in an airtight tin. They will keep for up to a week.

Palmiers are swirly cookies made from puff pastry. They look complicated to make, but in practice the process is pretty simple—just don't tell anyone else!

Chocolate Hazelnut Palmiers

MAKES 15

8 oz ready-made puff pastry
⅓ cup whole hazelnuts
2 teaspoons unsweetened cocoa
2 teaspoons stevia powder
  (see page 187)
pinch of ground mixed spice
all-purpose flour, for dusting
4 teaspoons unsalted butter, very
  soft, plus extra for greasing

Bring the pastry out of the refrigerator an hour before you want to use it to let it reach room temperature.

Preheat the oven to 400°F. Lightly grease a baking sheet with a little butter.

Place the hazelnuts, cocoa, stevia powder, and mixed spice in a food processor and pulse until you have a mixture with the texture of coffee grounds.

Roll out the pastry on a counter well dusted with flour to a rectangle about 8¾ x 12½ inches, and about 1/16 inch thick. Spread with 3 teaspoons of the butter. Sprinkle two-thirds of the nut mixture across.

With one long side nearest to you, imagine a vertical line down the center of your pastry. Fold either end of the pastry in to meet down the center, then spread the remaining butter across the resulting surface, followed by the rest of the nut mixture.

Fold each side in to meet down the center again. Finally, fold the left side over the right. You will now have a long, flattened sausage of folded pastry. Trim the ends to neaten and then cut into slices about ½ inch thick.

Lay the slices cut side up on the baking sheet, spacing them well apart as they will spread dramatically. Bake for 15–20 minutes until golden. Let cool on a wire rack. These are best eaten on the day they are made.

These voluminous scones are enriched with whole-wheat flour and naturally sweetened with rice milk. When served with a dollop of cream and some balsamic vinegar-infused strawberries, they'll not only give you that sweet treat you've been craving, but will also keep hunger pangs at bay.

Strawberry Scones

MAKES 8

generous 1¾ cups all-purpose flour, plus extra for dusting
scant ⅔ cup whole-wheat all-purpose flour
1 tablespoon baking powder
3½ tablespoons unsalted butter, chilled and cut into chunks, plus extra for greasing
½ cup rice milk
⅓ cup milk

For the topping
3½ cups fresh strawberries, hulled and thinly sliced
2 teaspoons balsamic vinegar
¼ teaspoon ground black pepper
1¼ cups whipping cream

Preheat the oven to 425°F. Lightly grease a baking sheet with a little butter.

Mix both flours and the baking powder together in a large bowl. Add the butter and rub in with your fingertips until the mixture resembles fine bread crumbs (you can pulse the ingredients in a food processor instead, if you prefer). Pour in the rice milk and milk. Stir everything together, then get your hands in and knead the mixture into a dough.

Roll out the dough on a counter well dusted with flour to a thickness of about 1¼ inches. Use a 2½ inch cookie cutter to cut out 8 circles, rerolling the trimmings as necessary, and place them on the baking sheet. Bake for 15 minutes until well risen and browned.

To make the topping, stir the strawberry slices, vinegar, and pepper together in a saucepan over medium heat for 5 minutes, taking care not to let the mixture boil. Once the strawberries have become softened and translucent and have released some of their juices, remove the saucepan from the heat and let everything cool. Whip the cream until it forms soft peaks.

Serve the scones cut in half, with each side topped by a dollop of whipped cream and a serving of the balsamic strawberries.

Cakes & Gateaux

In a very roundabout way, this cake was inspired by a recipe from British Michelin-starred chef Tom Kerridge. It uses tea to create an extra depth of flavor and a springy, moist texture. A wicked chocolate ganache finishes it off nicely.

Chocolate Tea Cake

MAKES ABOUT 12 SLICES

1 Earl Grey tea bag
3¾ oz pitted dried dates
scant ⅔ cup whole-wheat all-purpose flour
¼ cup unsweetened cocoa
7 tablespoons unsalted butter, very soft, plus extra for greasing
2 eggs
2 teaspoons baking powder
pinch of ground cloves
pinch of salt
2 oz no-added-sugar semisweet chocolate, plus extra for decorating

Use the tea bag to make a pot of tea, using about ⅔ cup boiling water and letting it brew for 5 minutes. Pour off the tea into a measuring cup, then soak the dates in ½ cup of the tea for at least 4 hours or overnight, setting aside the remaining tea for the ganache.

When the dates are softened and have absorbed most of the tea, preheat the oven to 350°F. Lightly grease a 8¾ x 4½ x 3 inch/2 lb loaf pan with a little butter.

Place the soaked dates and the tea they were soaking in in a food processor and process until smooth. Add the flour, cocoa, butter, eggs, baking powder, cloves, and salt and process for 3–4 seconds until everything has combined.

Scoop the cake batter into the pan and smooth the top with a spatula. Bake for 30 minutes until well risen and an inserted toothpick comes out clean. Let cool in the pan before removing and placing on a serving plate.

Meanwhile, make the ganache. Break up the chocolate into small pieces and place in a small saucepan with the reserved tea over low heat until the chocolate has melted, then stir well. Pour into a bowl and chill in the refrigerator for 30 minutes until the mixture has set. Spread it on the cooled cake. Use a vegetable peeler to create curls of chocolate and sprinkle over the top of the ganache to decorate. Eat within 2–3 days.

For this naturally gluten-free cake I've used the sunny Mediterranean flavors of apricots, almonds, and lemon. It uses pantry ingredients and its gentle fragrance and moist, chunky almonds help to make it a tempting prospect at any time of the year. Try it at teatime or as more of a dessert with a little crème fraîche.

Apricot & Lemon Cake

MAKES ABOUT 12 SLICES

scant 1½ cups soft dried apricots
2 cups whole almonds
generous 2 cups boiling water
sunflower oil, for oiling
juice and zest of ½ unwaxed lemon,
    plus extra zest
4 eggs
2 teaspoons baking powder
pinch of salt
12 blanched almonds
3 tablespoons fresh orange juice
crème fraîche, to serve

Set side scant ½ cup of the apricots. Place the remaining apricots in a bowl. Place the whole almonds in a separate bowl. Pour 1 cup boiling water into each bowl and let stand for 2 hours or overnight.

Preheat the oven to 350°F. Generously oil an 11 inch springform pan and line the bottom with parchment paper. Finely chop the reserved apricots.

Drain the soaked almonds and apricots and place them in a food processor with the lemon juice and zest, eggs, baking powder, and salt. Blend for about 1 minute until the almonds are finely ground. Stir in the chopped apricots, then transfer the mixture to the pan. Arrange the blanched almonds on top.

Bake for 30 minutes, then cover with foil, reduce the heat to 325°F, and bake for another 10 minutes. An inserted toothpick should come out clean.

Let the cake cool in the pan. Run a blunt knife around the edge before unclipping the pan. Transfer to a serving plate. Drizzle the orange juice over the top and let stand for 10 minutes before serving with a little crème fraîche topped with lemon zest.

Flavors of blackstrap molasses and toffee permeate this soft, moist cake. It is based on an Omani recipe, and though it is rather laden with dates, the small portion size keeps the sugar per slice to a minimum. I eat this cake cold as a midmorning treat, but it would also be fabulous served warm with custard.

Sticky Date & Apple Cake

MAKES 25 PIECES

1 large dessert apple, about 7 oz, plus 1 extra, about 5 oz, for decorating

8 oz pitted dried dates

1 cup water

7 tablespoons unsalted butter, plus extra for greasing

1 teaspoon baking soda

2 eggs

scant 1¼ cups whole-wheat all-purpose flour

2 teaspoons baking powder

1 teaspoon unsweetened vanilla extract

Preheat the oven to 400°F. Lightly grease an 8 inch square baking pan with a little butter.

Core the large apple (leave the skin on) and chop it coarsely into pieces about 1 inch in size. Place them in a saucepan with the dates and measurement water and bring to a boil. Boil the mixture for about 3 minutes until the apple is soft.

Meanwhile, quarter and core the smaller apple for decorating the cake (leave the skin), then cut it into thin slices and set aside.

Take the pan off the heat, then stir in the butter and let it melt. Next, stir in the baking soda. It will foam up rather impressively.

Place the eggs, flour, baking powder, and vanilla extract in a food processor. Add the foamy date mixture and blend for about 5 seconds until everything has combined.

Pour the cake batter into the pan and gently smooth the top with a spatula. Arrange the sliced apple decoratively on top—I prefer a Modernist esthetic, with the slices arranged in rows, but it's entirely up to you!

Bake for 40 minutes until the cake has risen and the edges are pulling away from the sides of the pan, and an inserted toothpick comes out clean. Let it cool in the pan before cutting it into 25 pieces. Eat within 2–3 days.

Variation

You can easily make a dairy-free version of this cake by using dairy-free margarine in place of the butter.

This is a rich, moist fruit cake made using nutritious whole-wheat flour, packed with raisins and apricots, and topped with whole almonds.

Fruit Cake

MAKES 8 SLICES

¼ cup dried apricots, finely chopped
1 cup raisins
¼ cup golden raisins
2½ teaspoons ground mixed spice
grated rind and juice 1 large
    unwaxed orange
2 bananas, about 8 oz total weight
3½ tablespoons butter, softened,
    plus extra for greasing
generous ¾ cup whole-wheat all-
    purpose flour
½ cup ground almonds
2 teaspoons baking powder
1 egg, beaten
½ cup whole almonds

Preheat the oven to 325°F. Lightly grease a deep 7 inch round cake pan with a little butter, then place the pan on a sheet of parchment paper and draw around it. Cut out the circle of parchment paper and lay on the bottom of the pan.

Place all the dried fruit, mixed spice, and orange rind in a bowl and stir to coat the fruit in the spice.

Peel and mash the bananas, then mix into the softened butter in a large bowl. Stir in the flour, ground almonds, baking powder, and egg until you have a paste.

Make up the orange juice in a measuring cup to ½ cup with water if necessary and stir into the cake batter. Now add the spiced fruit mixture and then stir well.

Scoop the cake batter into the pan and smooth the top with a spatula. Use the whole almonds to decorate the top.

Bake for 1 hour 40 minutes (don't open the door!) until the cake is well browned and an inserted toothpick comes out clean. Let cool in the pan, then run a blunt knife around the edge before carefully turning the pan upside down to remove the cake. This cake is best eaten within a week.

Variation

Make this cake dairy free by using dairy-free margarine in place of the butter.

Tip

If you don't have any mixed spice, you can use a mixture of 1 teaspoon ground cinnamon, 1 teaspoon ground coriander, ¼ teaspoon ground nutmeg, and ¼ teaspoon ground cloves instead.

The colorful nectarine slices are embedded within the soft vanilla sponge of this cake, making it not only attractive but also providing a lovely burst of sweetness. This cake works well both warm or cold, and if you want to make it more of a dessert, try it with some of my Vanilla Ice Cream (see page 89).

Nectarine Upside Down Cake

MAKES ABOUT 8 SLICES

scant ½ cup soft dried apricots
2 fresh nectarines
generous ¾ cup all-purpose flour
generous ¾ cup ground almonds
1⅜ sticks unsalted butter, very soft, plus extra for greasing
2 teaspoons baking powder
1 teaspoon unsweetened vanilla extract
4 eggs
1 teaspoon ground cinnamon, plus extra for dusting

Place the dried apricots in a mug and cover with boiling water. Let them soak for about 15 minutes.

Meanwhile, preheat the oven to 350°F. Lightly grease an 8 inch springform pan with a little butter.

Working over a bowl to catch the juice, slice the nectarines in half and remove the pit, then cut each half into about 8 segments. Arrange the segments decoratively across the bottom of the cake pan, aiming to cover as much of it as possible.

Drain the soaked dried apricots and place them in a food processor with all the remaining ingredients, including any juice reserved from preparing the nectarines. Process the mixture for about 10–15 seconds until you have a smooth cake batter. Pour it on top of the nectarine slices and gently smooth the top with a spatula.

Bake the cake for 30 minutes until risen and golden brown, and an inserted toothpick comes out clean. Let the cake cool in the pan for about 5 minutes, then run a blunt knife around the outside of the cake, place an upturned serving plate on top, and carefully flip both over together. Remove the pan to reveal your cake. Dust it with cinnamon to serve. Store the finished cake in the refrigerator and eat within a couple of days—it actually tastes better a day after it is made.

This is goodness in cake form, packed with butternut squash, dates, and apricots. It tastes best the day after it is made, so it's perfect for when you want to get things done in advance.

Spicy Ginger Cake with Apricot Topping

MAKES 16 SQUARES

For the cake
5 oz butternut squash
2 teaspoons sunflower oil, plus extra
   for oiling
5 tablespoons unsalted butter,
   melted
3½ oz pitted dried dates
½ cup milk
2 teaspoons ground ginger
1 teaspoon ground cinnamon
grated rind of 1 large unwaxed
   orange
1⅔ cups all-purpose flour
2 teaspoons baking powder
1 egg, beaten

For the topping
3½ tablespoons unsweetened
   smooth cashew nut butter
2 tablespoons salted butter, very soft
scant ½ cup soft dried apricots,
   finely chopped
1½ tablespoons raw unsalted
   cashew nuts, finely chopped

Preheat the oven to 400°F. Lightly oil an 8 inch square pan with a little sunflower oil.

Seed the butternut squash (keep the skin on) and cut into pieces about ½ inch square, then toss them in the oil in a roasting pan. Roast for 20 minutes until cooked through but only just browned. Remove them from the oven and let cool for about 5 minutes.

Place the roasted squash in a food processor with the melted butter, dates, milk, spices, and orange rind. Process until nearly smooth. Stir in the flour, baking powder, and egg.

Transfer the mixture to the pan, smooth the top with a spatula, and bake for 20–30 minutes. Let cool in the pan.

To make the topping, beat the cashew nut butter and butter together. Spread the mixture across the top of the cooled cake, then sprinkle the apricot and cashews across the nut paste. Chill the cake in the refrigerator for an hour until the topping has set, then cut into 16 squares. This cake will keep for 2–3 days.

Variation

Use dairy-free margarine in place of butter and soy milk in place of milk to create a dairy-free version of this recipe.

This is a fabulously moist, spiced carrot cake, with natural sweetness provided not only by the carrot and raisins but also by the generous quantity of dreamy, orange-flavored frosting.

Carrot Cake

MAKES ABOUT 12 SLICES

For the cake
1½ cups walnuts, chopped
1⅔ cups finely shredded carrot
1¼ cups whole-wheat all-purpose
   flour
2 teaspoons ground cinnamon
¼ teaspoon ground cloves
2 teaspoons baking powder
½ teaspoon baking soda
½ cup sunflower oil, plus extra
   for oiling
1 cup milk
2 eggs, beaten
2 tablespoons stevia powder (see
   page 187)
1 tablespoon fresh orange juice
scant ½ cup golden raisins

For the frosting
⅓ cup whipping cream
scant ⅔ cup cream cheese
1 tablespoon stevia powder (see
   page 187)
1 tablespoon fresh orange juice
grated rind of 1 unwaxed orange,
   plus extra for decorating
2 tablespoons chopped walnuts

Preheat the oven to 350°F. Lightly oil an 8¾ x 4½ x 3 inch/2 lb loaf pan with a little sunflower oil.

....

Place 1 cup of the walnut pieces in a food processor and process them to the texture of coarse coffee grounds. Transfer to a bowl and add the shredded carrot, flour, spices, baking powder, and baking soda. Give everything a good stir.

....

Mix the oil, milk, eggs, stevia powder, and orange juice together in a small bowl. Pour the liquid mixture into the bowl with the other ingredients and stir quickly until everything is combined. Add the golden raisins and remainder of the walnuts, give another quick stir, and then pour the cake batter into the loaf pan. Smooth the top with a spatula.

....

Bake the loaf for 45–50 minutes until browned and risen, and an inserted toothpick comes out clean. Let the cake cool in the pan.

....

To make the frosting, whip the cream until it forms soft peaks and then beat in the cream cheese. Stir the stevia powder into the orange juice in a small bowl until it has dissolved and then pour it into the cream cheese mixture. Add the grated rind and fold everything together with a spatula.

....

Remove the cake from the pan. Smear the cream cheese mixture across the top, then use a fork to make a decorative pattern. Finish by sprinkling the chopped walnuts across the top, along with a little extra grated rind. Store the finished cake in the refrigerator and eat within a couple of days.

Gateau Marcel is a two-tier chocolate mousse, one raw and one baked into a soft cake. Invented by the Michelin-starred chef Michel Michaud, this indulgent and gluten-free creation is easy to make, although it does need to be prepared in advance.

Gateau Marcel with Cherries & Blueberries

SERVES 6–8

sunflower oil, for oiling
3½ oz no-added-sugar semisweet chocolate, broken into small pieces
2 oz no-added-sugar milk chocolate, broken into small pieces
1⅜ sticks unsalted butter, chopped
pinch of fine salt
2 eggs
3 egg whites
5 oz fresh black cherries, pitted and halved
½ cup fresh blueberries

Preheat the oven to 350°F. Line the bottom of an 8 inch square cake pan with parchment paper and lightly oil the sides with a little sunflower oil.

Place the chocolates and butter with the salt in a saucepan over low heat until they have melted, stirring occasionally.

Separate the whole eggs. Place all the whites in a medium bowl and the yolks in a large bowl.

Using an electric whisk, whisk the whites until very stiff—you will have reached the right level of stiffness if they won't move when the bowl is tipped to the side.

Use the whisk to whisk the yolks until they have turned a few shades paler and become fluffy. While continuing to whisk, very slowly pour in the hot chocolate mixture in a thin stream. You'll be left with a thick and glossy chocolate paste.

Fold the whisked egg whites into the chocolate paste. When everything has been combined and you have a mousse, pour half the batter into the cake pan. Bake for 20 minutes until puffy.

Let the cake cool in the pan (it will sink significantly), then pour the remaining chocolate mousse on top of the cake. Place in the refrigerator for at least 4 hours until set.

When you are ready to serve, run a blunt knife around the edge of the gateau and lift it out of the pan. Remove the lining paper. Place the gateau on a serving plate. Sprinkle the cherries and blueberries across the top of the gateau.

Tip

If you have egg yolks left over after making this recipe, consider using them to make the Portuguese Custard Tarts (see page 58), Vanilla Ice Cream (see page 89), or Chocolate Chip Ice Cream (see page 89).

There's a hint of tiramisu flavoring in this light sponge cake, which is filled with a rich and creamy chestnut and prune center. A dusting of cocoa finishes everything off nicely.

Chestnut Tiramisu Cake

SERVES 8–12

For the sponge
sunflower oil, for oiling
6 eggs
1⅓ cups chestnut flour
pinch of salt
4 tablespoons freshly made strong
    coffee, cooled
2 tablespoons white rum (optional)

For the filling and decoration
3½ oz pitted prunes
⅓ cup boiling water
2 teaspoons unsweetened vanilla
    extract
2 teaspoons stevia powder (see
    page 187)
1⅔ cups whipping cream
7 oz unsweetened chestnut puree
2 teaspoons unsweetened cocoa,
    for dusting

Before you start, soak the prunes for the filling and decoration in the measurement boiling water, ideally for a minimum of 2 hours.

Preheat the oven to 350°F. Lightly oil two 8 inch sandwich pans with a little sunflower oil, then place one pan on a double-thickness sheet of parchment paper and draw around it. Cut out the circles of parchment paper and lay one on the bottom of each pan.

To make the sponge, separate the eggs and place the whites in a large bowl and the yolks in a separate bowl.

Using an electric whisk, whisk the whites until very stiff—they shouldn't move when the bowl is tipped to the side.

Whisk the yolks until they have turned a few shades paler and become fluffy. Fold into the whisked egg white, followed by the chestnut flour and salt.

When everything is well combined, divide the batter between the pans and bake for 15 minutes until just browned. Let the sponges cool in the pans.

For the filling, place the softened prunes and their soaking water in a blender and blend to a puree, then set aside.

Stir the vanilla extract and stevia powder together in a small bowl until the stevia has dissolved. Pour into a large bowl with the cream. Whip the cream until it forms firm peaks, then fold in the chestnut puree.

Now it's time to assemble your cake. Place the first sponge layer on a serving plate. Stir the coffee and rum together, if using. Pour half across the sponge layer, followed by one-third of the cream mixture, spreading it evenly across the sponge base. Spread the prune puree on top.

Add the second sponge layer and drench it with the remaining coffee mixture, followed by another one-third of the cream. Pipe the remaining cream around the sides of the cake. Dust the top with the cocoa and serve. Store in the refrigerator and eat within a couple of days.

This German-style cake is topped with juicy pears and slivered almonds. I've used canned pears for ease, but peeled, ripe dessert pears would make a wonderful alternative.

Pear Kuchen

MAKES 9 PIECES

½ cup milk, plus
   1 tablespoon for glazing
1 teaspoon unsweetened vanilla
   extract
1 tablespoon stevia powder (see
   page 187)
2 tablespoons salted butter,
   chopped, plus extra for greasing
1 teaspoon active dry yeast
1¼ cups all-purpose flour
½ cup ground almonds
1 egg, beaten
7½ oz drained canned pear halves
   in fruit juice
1 tablespoon slivered almonds

Lightly grease an 8 inch square cake pan with a little butter.

Heat the milk with the vanilla extract and stevia powder in a saucepan. Just before it starts to boil, take the pan off the heat, add the butter, and let it melt. When the liquid has cooled to hand-hot, stir in the yeast.

Mix the flour and ground almonds together in a bowl. Pour the milk mixture and egg into the bowl, and stir to combine everything into a soft, sticky dough.

Press the dough into the pan, using the back of a spoon to ease it into the corners and to create an even layer. Leave it under a clean damp dish towel somewhere warm for an hour or so until it looks puffy.

Preheat the oven to 400°F. Cut each pear half into 6 slices and arrange them on the top of the dough. Brush all the exposed dough with the remaining tablespoon of milk and sprinkle over the slivered almonds.

Bake for 25 minutes until the dough has risen and become golden. Cut into 9 pieces, then let cool for a while in the pan and serve warm.
This is best eaten the same day.

I love the dramatic color contrast of red velvet cake and this recipe gives a moist and moreish result, yet it's packed with goodness, so different from store-bought versions! Of course, no red velvet cake would be worth its name without a wicked cream cheese frosting, so there is plenty of that too.

Red Velvet Cake

SERVES 8–12

For the cake
8 oz fresh beet
1¼ cups whole-wheat
   all-purpose flour
1¼ cups white all-purpose flour
4 teaspoons baking powder
1 tablespoon unsweetened cocoa
1 cup sunflower oil, plus extra
   for oiling
¾ cup milk
⅓ cup plain yogurt
4 tablespoons freshly made strong
   coffee, cooled
2 eggs
4 tablespoons stevia powder (see
   page 187)
2 teaspoons unsweetened vanilla
   extract
2 teaspoons red food coloring
   (optional)
1 teaspoon balsamic vinegar

For the frosting
1⅔ cups whipping cream
⅔ cup cream cheese
3 teaspoons unsweetened vanilla
   extract
2 tablespoons stevia powder
   (see page 187)

Preheat the oven to 350°F. Lightly oil two 8 inch sandwich pans with a little sunflower oil and line the bottoms with nonstick parchment paper.

Finely grate the beet into a large bowl and add both flours, the baking powder, and cocoa. Mix all the remaining cake ingredients together in a separate bowl. Pour the liquid mixture into the beet mixture and stir quickly until you have a sloppy pink batter. Divide it evenly between the cake pans.

Bake the cakes for 40 minutes until risen and browned, and an inserted toothpick comes out clean. Remove the cakes from their pans and let them cool upside down on a wire rack.

To make the frosting, whip the cream until it forms soft peaks, then whisk in the cream cheese. Stir the vanilla extract and stevia powder together until the stevia has dissolved, then add to the cream cheese mixture. Whip briefly until everything is combined.

To assemble the cake, place the first cake layer on a serving plate and spread half the frosting across it. Add the second cake layer, followed by the remaining frosting. Use a fork to add a few decorative swirls to the frosting. Keep the finished cake in the refrigerator until ready to serve. Eat within a couple of days.

These tarts are known as pasteis de nata and I became familiar with them after living in London's "little Portugal" district. They can be tricky to make at home (the recipe originates from a Lisbon café that has an extremely hot oven), but by using my technique it is possible to achieve great results.

Portuguese Custard Tarts

MAKES 12

butter, for greasing
10 oz ready-made puff pastry
⅓ cup milk
1 tablespoon all-purpose flour,
    plus extra for dusting
2 egg yolks
2 eggs, beaten
¾ cup rice milk
2 teaspoons stevia powder
    (see page 187)
1 teaspoon unsweetened vanilla
    extract
½ teaspoon ground cinnamon,
    for dusting

Bring the pastry out of the refrigerator an hour before you want to use it to let it reach room temperature.

Preheat the oven to 475°F. Grease the sections of a 12-section muffin pan with butter.

Roll out the pastry on a counter well dusted with flour to a rectangle about 6¾ x 5 inches, and about ½ inch thick, but don't worry if you accidentally make it a little larger than this. Brush the top with water and then, starting from one short side, roll it up tightly. You'll now have a cylinder of pastry.

Trim the ends of the pastry cylinder to neaten it, then cut it into 4 equal lengths and cut each length into 3 slices. With the cut side uppermost, roll your rolling pin over each slice a couple of times so that you get a rough circle about 3 inches in diameter. Place a pastry circle into each section of the muffin pan and use your fingertips to stretch the pastry until you have lined each section and there are no gaps.

For the filling, stir the milk and flour together in a bowl until smooth. Beat the egg yolks and whole eggs together in a separate bowl and set 1 tablespoon aside. Pour the remaining egg into the milk. Add the rice milk, stevia powder, and vanilla extract and whisk until everything is combined.

Pour the filling into the pastry shells, dividing the mixture evenly between them. Brush the exposed pastry with the reserved egg.

Bake the custard tarts for 15 minutes until the filling has risen and has brown spots. Let the tarts cool in the pan for about 10 minutes—the filling will sink down as they do so. Dust a little of the cinnamon over each one and then serve. These are best eaten the same day.

Tip
If you have egg whites left over, why not use them to make my Gateau Marcel (see page 53)?

These simple fruit tarts are fresh and easy, and are a great idea for an elegant event—sprinkled with edible flowers, they'll easily be the star attraction.

Raspberry Tarts

MAKES 4

sunflower oil, for oiling
all-purpose flour, for dusting
1 quantity of Low-Carb Dessert
    Dough (see page 170)
½ cup whipping cream
1 large ripe dessert pear, about 6 oz,
    peeled and cored
2¼ cups fresh raspberries
handful of edible flower petals, such
    as viola or dianthus (optional)

Preheat the oven to 400°F. Lightly oil four 4 inch round fluted tart pans with a little sunflower oil.

Roll out the pastry on a counter well dusted with flour to a thickness of about ⅛ inch. Roughly cut out 4 circles slightly larger than the pans. Press each pastry circle into a pan and trim the excess with a sharp knife.

Place a layer of foil over the top of each pastry shell, then fill with dried beans or pie weights. Bake for 20 minutes until the pastry is crisp and just turning golden brown. Let the pastry shells cool in the pans and then lift the beans and foil out.

Just before you want to serve your tarts, remove the pastry shells from the pans and place them on a serving plate. Whip the cream until it forms soft peaks. Place the pear in a separate bowl and use an immersion blender to puree it, then fold it into the cream. Spread the cream mixture evenly across each of the tarts and arrange the raspberries on top. Finish with a sprinkling of edible flower petals, if desired. These are best eaten immediately.

Desserts

This sunset-colored gelatin dessert is made with fresh juices and studded with pomegranate seeds. Serve with cream or my Vanilla Ice Cream (see page 89).

Clementine & Pomegranate Dessert

SERVES 4

10 clementines, about 1½ lb total weight
2 pomegranates
2 tablespoons white wine
5 leaves of gelatin

First, thoroughly juice the clementines into a measuring cup and set aside. Pomegranates can be messy, but there is a simple way to extract the juice. Score a line all the way around each pomegranate with a knife. Now score a second line at a right angle to the first. Fill a large bowl with water and hold one pomegranate underneath the water. Pull it apart along the scored lines, then loosen all the seeds. The white pith should float to the surface while the seeds sink. Using a slotted spoon, fish out as much of the pith as you can, then pour the contents of the bowl through a colander. You will be left with the seeds. Repeat the process for the second pomegranate. Take one-quarter of the seeds and sprinkle them in the bottom of a 20 oz jelly mold or 4 individual 5 oz jelly molds.

Place the remaining pomegranate seeds in a plastic tub. Using the back of a tablespoon, press down on each seed until it is squashed flat and the juice has come out. Strain the mixture through a strainer into the clementine juice. You will now have a beautiful pinkish orange liquid. Add the wine and, if necessary, make up the quantity of liquid to generous 2 cups with water.

Place the leaves of gelatin in a bowl and cover with cold water. Let soak for 5 minutes so that they become really floppy, then transfer them to a small saucepan and heat very gently until they melt. Add the juice to the pan and stir until everything is combined.

Pour the juice mixture into the jelly mold and refrigerate overnight.

To serve, place the mold in a bowl of hand-hot water (don't let the water come over the sides of the jelly mold) until the edges of the jelly have melted very slightly. This will happen very quickly for metal molds, but will be slower with plastic molds. Place an upturned serving dish on top of the mold, then flip both over together, give a quick shake and remove the mold. Serve immediately.

Variation

To make a vegetarian/vegan version of this recipe, stir 1 tablespoon agar powder (see page 186) into 4 tablespoons of the clementine juice in a small saucepan and heat gently until it has dissolved. Pour in the remaining liquid (make sure the wine is suitable for vegans, if necessary) and make up to generous 2 cups with water if necessary. Pour the juice mixture into the mold with the pomegranate seeds as detailed above, then chill in the refrigerator for a couple of hours before serving.

Crisp, fresh red grapes are the secret to this tart's success—
not only are they a wonderful counterbalance to the seductive
chocolate filling, they also give the tart its distinctive jewel-like
appearance. This tastes great served with cream.

Jeweled Chocolate Tart

SERVES 6–8

butter, for greasing
all-purpose flour, for dusting
1 quantity of Low-Carb Dessert
    Dough (see page 170)
5 oz no-added-sugar semisweet
    chocolate, broken into small
    pieces
generous ¾ cup heavy cream
4 eggs
10 oz red seedless grapes
1 teaspoon red wine
½ teaspoon raw local honey

Preheat the oven to 400°F. Lightly grease an 8 inch tart pan with a
little butter.

....

Roll out the dough on a counter well dusted with flour to a thickness of
about ⅛ inch. Roughly cut out a circle slightly larger than the pan. Press
the dough into the pan and trim the excess with a sharp knife. Set the
pastry shell aside.

....

Place the chocolate with the cream in a saucepan over low heat until it has
melted, stirring occasionally. Whisk the eggs together in a bowl for 8–10
minutes until doubled in volume and pale in color. While continuing to
whisk, very slowly pour in the hot chocolate mixture in a thin stream. You
will end up with a dark chocolaty custard. Pour it into the pastry shell.

....

Bake the tart for 40–45 minutes until the filling has puffed up all over and
taken on a cracked appearance. Remove from the oven.

....

While the tart cools a little, use paper towels to polish the grapes and
remove the bloom. Slice the grapes in half. I like to slice some vertically
and some horizontally to give greater scope for creativity in decorating
the tart. Arrange the grapes in concentric circles across the top of the
chocolate filling.

....

Stir the wine and honey together in a cup to create a glaze. Brush the
grapes with the red wine mixture and then serve immediately.

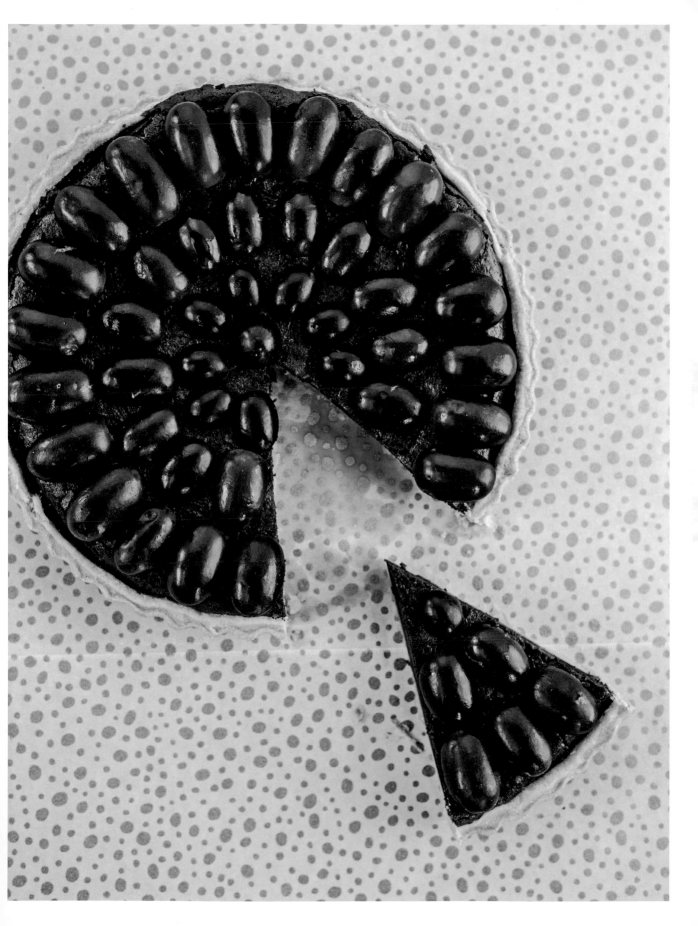

Evaporated milk is a very underrated ingredient with a distinctive flavor and delicate sweetness. It goes brilliantly with cream cheese and mandarin oranges in this retro chilled cheesecake. If you can't find oatcakes, use whole-wheat savory crackers instead.

Mandarin Cheesecake

SERVES 6–8

For the base
4 oz unsweetened oatcakes
3½ tablespoons unsalted butter, melted
2 teaspoons stevia powder (see page 187)
½ teaspoon ground ginger

For the topping
3 leaves of gelatin
1 cup whipping cream
1 cup cream cheese
⅓ cup evaporated milk
1 teaspoon stevia powder (see page 187)
2 (10 oz) cans mandarin orange segments in juice

Bash the oatcakes into crumbs by placing them in a sealed plastic food bag and hitting with a rolling pin. Alternatively, blitz them in a food processor. Stir the melted butter into the crumb mixture with the stevia powder and ginger. Tip the crumb mixture into a deep 8 inch loose-bottom tart pan and then use the back of a metal tablespoon to gently stroke the mixture until it is smooth and evenly distributed. Chill in the refrigerator for at least an hour until the butter has set.

To make the topping, place the leaves of gelatin in a bowl and cover with cold water. Let soak for 5 minutes so that they become really floppy. Meanwhile, whip the cream until it forms firm peaks. Add the cream cheese, evaporated milk, and stevia powder and whip until you have a smooth, somewhat sloppy mixture.

Drain one can of mandarin segments and place 4 tablespoons of the juice in a small saucepan. Add the softened gelatin leaves and heat very gently until they melt. Pour the gelatin mixture into the cream cheese mixture and whip briefly. Pour onto the prepared cookie base and put the pan back in the refrigerator for at least 2 hours.

Just before serving, drain the second can of mandarin segments. Decoratively arrange the segments from both cans on the top of the cheesecake. Release the cheesecake from the pan and serve.

Variation

Use gluten-free crackers for a gluten-free version of this dessert.

This chilled dessert combines a variety of Mediterranean flavors in an unusual yet delightful way. I tried something similar in a Copenhagen restaurant some years ago and totally fell in love with it. The almond rice is gently sweetened with rice milk, while the balsamic figs give an amazing burst of flavor—but do start soaking them the day before, if you can.

Creamy Almond Rice with Balsamic Figs

SERVES 4–6

For the balsamic figs
7 oz soft dried figs
¾ cup boiling water
1 tablespoon balsamic vinegar

For the almond rice
½ cup short-grain rice
generous 2 cups rice milk
2 tablespoons sherry or vermouth
1⅔ cups whipping cream
¾ cup whole blanched almonds, finely chopped

Remove the tough stalky part at the top of each fig, then cut each fig into 5 or 6 slices and place in a bowl with the measurement boiling water and balsamic vinegar. Let soak for at least 4 hours, or preferably overnight.

Place the rice and rice milk in a saucepan and bring to a boil, then reduce the heat and simmer for about 15 minutes until the rice is tender and almost all the liquid has been absorbed. Stir in the sherry or vermouth, then let the mixture cool completely. It will become really stodgy and rather solid, but this is fine.

Whip the cream until it forms firm peaks. Add to the cooled rice with the almonds and fold everything together until well combined. Serve each portion of almond rice topped with the balsamic figs.

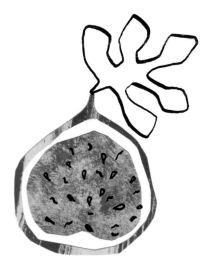

These pears not only turn a dark pink during their gentle poaching in spiced wine but also take on a buttery smoothness. They are fantastic eaten with the cool and creamy mascarpone. This dish works best with slightly underripe pears of an even shape and size. Serve hot or cold.

Poached Pears with Mascarpone

SERVES 4

4 firm Bosc pears, about 6 oz each
1 cup red wine
1 cup water
1 cinnamon stick
4 cloves
grated rind of ½ unwaxed lemon
1 cup mascarpone cheese

For the sauce
1 ripe pear
1 teaspoon cornstarch
2 teaspoons water

Variation

Serve with soy cream in place of the mascarpone to make this recipe vegan and dairy free.

Peel the 4 pears but leave them whole. Lay them sideways in a deep 6¼ inch pan—it will be a bit of a squeeze, but they should all fit in. Pour over the wine and measurement water until the pears are nearly submerged. Add the whole spices and lemon rind.

Heat the pears over low heat for 40 minutes. After about 20 minutes, use a spoon to turn the pears gently to ensure even coloration. Strain the liquid from the pears into a bowl, then set aside ½ cup of it and discard the rest along with the spices.

To make the sauce, peel the pear and remove the core. Place in a blender with the reserved poaching liquid and blend to a puree. Strain the puree through a strainer into a saucepan over low heat.

Mix the cornstarch with the measurement water in a cup until smooth. Stir into the wine and pear mixture, then heat gently, stirring continuously, until boiling and thickened.

Cut a sliver off the base of each whole pear to enable them to sit upright on their serving plate. Finish by adding a dollop of the mascarpone, surrounded by a swirl of the sauce.

The fruitiness of the prunes lends an extra dimension to the flavor of the chocolate, meaning this irresistible mousse is rich in taste yet has a wonderfully light consistency. Serve in elegant stemmed glasses to make it extra special.

Chocolate Mousse

SERVES 4

3½ oz pitted prunes
4 tablespoons water
3 teaspoons amaretto
1 oz no-added-sugar semisweet
chocolate, broken into small
pieces, plus extra for decorating
½ cup sour cream
¼ cup unsweetened cocoa
4 egg whites
pinch of salt

Soak the prunes in the measurement water and amaretto for about 4 hours. After this time, strain any remaining liquid into a small saucepan and add the chocolate. Stir gently over low heat until the chocolate has melted.

Place the prunes, melted chocolate mixture, sour cream, and cocoa in a blender and blend until you have a thick, smooth paste. Transfer it to a large bowl.

Using an electric whisk, whisk the egg whites with the salt until very stiff —you will have reached the right level of stiffness if they won't move when the bowl is tipped to the side. Gently fold into the chocolate prune mixture until everything is evenly combined.

Divide the mixture between 4 dessert glasses. Smooth the top of each portion using a blunt knife. Finally, grate a little extra chocolate over the top. Chill in the refrigerator for at least an hour before serving.

Variation

For a different slant on this recipe and to make it nut free, use whisky in place of the amaretto.

Thinly sliced apples, fried in butter, are then cooked in a whisky-flavored almond batter—basically, it's a dessert version of the classic Spanish tortilla. Serve it hot, with crème fraîche or my Vanilla Ice Cream (see page 89).

Apple Tortilla

SERVES 4

4 dessert apples, about 1¼ lb
total weight
2 tablespoons unsalted butter
4 eggs
½ cup ground almonds
4 tablespoons sour cream
4 tablespoons milk
2 tablespoons whisky
2 teaspoons stevia powder
(see page 187)
½ teaspoon unsweetened vanilla
extract

Cut the apples into quarters, remove the cores (leave the skin on), and then slice them very thinly. Melt the butter in a 12 inch skillet and fry the apple slices over low heat, to prevent them burning, for about 10 minutes until soft.

Meanwhile, whisk all the remaining ingredients together in a bowl. Pour the mixture over the softened apples and then leave the pan on medium to medium-low heat for about 30 minutes until the surface of the mixture loses its gloss and has set. Cut the tortilla into slices and serve immediately.

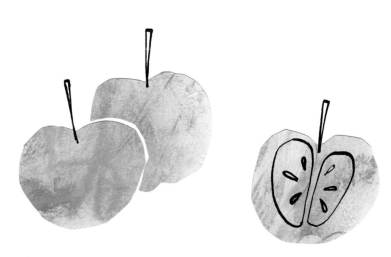

A roulade is not difficult to make but always looks impressive, so it's a win-win situation. This one is filled with cream sweetened with banana, while passion fruit adds a zingy, acidic bite that totally lifts the overall dessert.

Tropical Roulade

SERVES 8

For the sponge
1 banana, about 7 oz
4 eggs
generous ¾ cup all-purpose flour

For the filling
1¼ cups whipping cream
2 bananas, about 13 oz total weight
6 passion fruit

Preheat the oven to 425°F. Line a 14 x 11 inch baking pan with silicone parchment paper.

Peel and mash the banana in a large bowl. Separate the eggs and add the yolks to the banana and place the whites in a medium bowl. Using an electric whisk, whisk the egg whites until very stiff—you will have reached the right level of stiffness if they won't move when the bowl is tipped to the side.

Whisk the yolks and banana together until you have a foamy mixture. Sift the flour on top of the yolks, then spoon the whisked whites on top of the flour. Gently fold everything together until well combined.

Gently spread the batter evenly across the parchment paper in the baking pan. Bake for 10 minutes until golden brown. Lift the sponge out of the baking pan using the lining paper. With the paper still in place and using a clean dish towel to hold the sponge, roll it up, starting from one short edge, into a cylinder. Let it cool completely.

Just before you want to eat, make the filling. Whip the cream until it forms firm peaks. Peel and mash one of the bananas, then fold into the cream. Peel and finely slice the second banana. Cut the passion fruit in half and scoop out the seeds and pulp. Set aside some of the fruit for decoration. Gently unroll the sponge cylinder and spread it with two-thirds of the cream mixture. Sprinkle the banana slices and passion fruit seeds and pulp across the cream. Roll the sponge up again, gently peeling off the lining paper as you do so.

Place the finished roulade seam down and trim the ends to neaten it. Spread the the top with the remaining cream mixture. Top with the reserved banana and passion fruit. Cut it into slices and serve immediately.

Ripe, juicy plums have a wonderful natural sweetness that marries well with the toasted almonds and cinnamon in these simple tarts. Serve with whipped cream or crème fraîche.

Plum Tarts

MAKES 6

5 oz ready-made puff pastry
sunflower oil, for oiling
all-purpose flour, for dusting
3 teaspoons milk
¼ cup slivered almonds
4 ripe plums, about 8 oz total weight
½ teaspoon ground cinnamon

Bring the pastry out of the refrigerator an hour before you want to use it to let it reach room temperature.

Preheat the oven to 400°F. Lightly oil a baking sheet with a little sunflower oil.

Roll out the pastry on a counter well dusted with flour to a thickness of about ⅛ inch. Use a 3½ inch round cookie cutter, or the top of a mug or similar as a guide, to cut out 6 circles and place them on the baking sheet, rerolling the trimmings as necessary. Use a slightly smaller cutter, or mug, about 2½ inches in diameter, and lightly press it into the center of each of your pastry circles without cutting all the way through the pastry. Bake for 15 minutes until puffed and golden.

While the pastry is baking, toast the almonds in a dry skillet until browned. Cut the plums in half and remove the pits, then chop the plums into small pieces, about ½ inch in size.

Remove the pastry from the oven. Push down the central circle of each pastry circle to create a mini tart shell with a raised pastry edge. Heap the chopped plums in the center of each one, then sprinkle over the toasted almonds and cinnamon. Pop the tarts back in the oven for 5 minutes to warm them through and then serve.

Glistening, crispy phyllo pastry parcels allow the juices from baked banana and orange to collect into pools of fragrant deliciousness. Serve these desserts hot with cream.

Banana & Orange Phyllo Parcels

MAKES 4

2 bananas, about 11 oz total weight
6 oz drained canned mandarins
5 sheets of ready-made phyllo pastry, about 3½ oz total weight
3½ tablespoons salted butter, melted

Preheat the oven to 400°F. Cut 4 pieces of foil roughly 6 inches square.

Peel the bananas and cut into medium slices. Chop the mandarins coarsely and set aside.

Lay your stack of phyllo pastry sheets lengthwise and cut it in half vertically and horizontally to create 4 rectangular piles. Leave them under a clean dish towel to prevent the pastry drying out.

Take your first pile of phyllo pastry rectangles and brush each sheet with melted butter. Place one-quarter of the banana slices and chopped mandarins in the center. Scrunch the edges of the pastry and bring them together to create a sack shape.

Place your parcel in the center of a foil square, then scrunch the edges of the foil together to support the pastry, taking care to leave an opening at the top. Place the finished parcel on a baking sheet. Repeat the process for the remaining 3 piles of phyllo pastry.

Brush any remaining butter across the visible surfaces of the pastry parcels. Bake for 20 minutes, then remove the baking sheet from the oven and push all the foil flat. Place the parcels back in the oven for another 15 minutes until they are golden brown all over. Serve immediately.

A sweet meringue tops a tangy and creamy pineapple filling in this fresh take on the classic lemon meringue pie.

Pineapple Meringue

SERVES 6–8

butter, for greasing
all-purpose flour, for dusting
9 oz ready-made unsweetened basic pie dough or 1 quantity of Low-Carb Dessert Dough (see page 170)
1 egg white, beaten
3 eggs
4 oz drained canned pineapple chunks, finely chopped
¾ cup pineapple juice
⅓ cup cornstarch
½ cup mascarpone cheese
pinch of salt
1 tablespoon stevia powder (see page 187)
1 tablespoon raw organic local honey

Preheat the oven to 400°F. Lightly grease an 8 inch tart pan with a little butter.

Roll out the pastry on a counter well dusted with flour to a thickness of about ⅛ inch. Roughly cut out a circle slightly larger than the pan. Press the pastry into the pan and trim the excess with a sharp knife. Chill in the refrigerator for 20 minutes. Place a sheet of parchment paper over the top of the tart shell, then fill with dried beans or pie weights. Bake for 15–20 minutes and then remove from the oven and lift the paper and beans out —the pastry should feel dry and sandy to the touch. Brush with the beaten egg white and return to the oven for 5 minutes, until dry and golden.

While the tart base is baking, separate the eggs and place the yolks in a small bowl and the whites in a large bowl. Set aside.

Remove the tart base from the oven and set aside. Sprinkle the pineapple chunks over a baking sheet and roast in the oven for 15 minutes to dry them out.

Stir the pineapple juice and cornstarch together in a small saucepan. Bring to a boil, whisking continuously. When you have a thick, translucent paste, remove the pan from the heat and whisk in the mascarpone and egg yolks, followed by the roasted pineapple chunks.

Pour in the mascarpone mixture into the pastry base and smooth it out.

Now make the meringue. Place the bowl with the egg whites on a large saucepan of simmering water, making sure the bowl does not touch the water. Using an electric whisk, whisk the egg whites with the salt, stevia powder, and honey until you have a dense white foam.

Gently spread the meringue across the top of the mascarpone mixture. To finish the top, use a mini blow torch or place under a preheated hot broiler for 1–2 minutes until the meringue has some color, if desired.

This fresh, breezy dessert is quick to make and is a sensationally sweet way to end a meal. Even better, it can be made a few hours in advance, but should be eaten on the day it is made.

Raspberry & Mint Sundae

SERVES 4

1 cup sour cream
scant 1¼ cups fresh raspberries
4½ oz red seedless grapes
2 teaspoons finely shredded mint

Line up your serving glasses and spoon out half the sour cream evenly between them.

Set aside 4 raspberries as decoration, then lightly mash the rest and spread them across the sour cream in the glasses. Chop each grape into quarters and distribute the pieces over the mashed raspberries. Add a sprinkling of mint to each glass, leaving a little for decoration.

Finish by spooning out the remaining sour cream. Pop a raspberry on the top of each dessert, followed by the remaining mint. Chill in the refrigerator until ready to serve.

Coconut water is the naturally sweet juice that comes from young tender, coconuts and it contains a unique mixture of nutrients. It's wonderful here, mixed with juicy peaches and crème fraîche.

Peach Fruit Fool

SERVES 4

1 cup coconut water
⅓ cup cornstarch
1 cup crème fraîche
5 ripe peaches

Whisk the coconut water and cornstarch together in a saucepan until smooth, then bring to a boil, whisking continuously. When the mixture has become translucent and thick, take it off the heat and let it cool completely, stirring occasionally. It will thicken more as it cools. Stir in the crème fraîche until well combined.

Cut 4 of the peaches in half and remove the pits. Dice the flesh into pieces not more than ½ inch square. Place them in a large bowl and spoon over the crème fraîche mixture. Stir everything together, and then chill in the refrigerator for an hour.

Just before serving, spoon the fool into serving bowls. Cut the remaining peach in half and remove the pit, then slice up and use to decorate the fools.

The delicate flavor of fresh figs takes center stage in this elegant dessert. The subtle creaminess makes the perfect finish to a spicy main course.

Fresh Fig Panna Cotta

SERVES 4

For the panna cotta
2–3 leaves of gelatin
1 cup milk
1 cup light cream
2 teaspoons white wine (optional)
½ teaspoon stevia powder (see page 187)

For the sauce
4 fresh figs, about 10 oz, plus 1 extra for decorating
4 red seedless grapes, plus 4 extra for decorating

Place the leaves of gelatin in a bowl and cover with cold water (use 3 leaves of gelatin if you prefer a firmer set). Let soak for 5 minutes so that they become really floppy.

Meanwhile, heat the milk and cream together in a saucepan until hot but not boiling.

Remove the pan from the heat and stir in the softened gelatin, wine (if using), and stevia powder. Pour the mixture into 4 dariole molds. Chill in the refrigerator for about 4 hours until set.

When you are ready to serve, make the sauce. Cut the figs in half, scoop out the flesh with a spoon, and place it in a blender with the grapes (for a smoother sauce, peel the grapes first). Blend briefly until there are no large lumps remaining.

Briefly dip each dariole mold into a bowl of hand-hot water to loosen the panna cotta, making sure that no water comes over the top of the mold. Place an upturned serving plate over the top of the mold, then flip both over together, giving one or two sharp shakes as you do so. The panna cotta should slide neatly out of its mold onto the plate.

Distribute the fig puree between the plates of panna cotta. To decorate, slice the extra fig and the grapes very thinly and arrange across each dessert. Serve immediately.

Don't be fooled by the simplicity of the ingredients of this
fruit salad because the taste is anything but. A combination
of sweet, sour, and perfume, it makes a wonderful conclusion
to a rich or spicy meal. This salad works best with the delicate
taste and low acidity of pink grapefruit.

Fragrant Fruit Salad

SERVES 4–6

2 ripe papayas
2 pink grapefruit
11½ oz fresh litchis
   or 2 (7 oz) cans litchis
   in juice
4 passion fruit

To prepare the papayas, cut them in half and scoop out the seeds with
a spoon, then remove the skin with a vegetable peeler. Slice the flesh into
roughly ¾ inch square pieces. Place all the pieces in a large serving bowl.

Working over the bowl to catch the juice, prepare the grapefruit by cutting
the rind and white pith off with a paring knife, then slicing either side of
each segment to free them from the skin. Cut each segment in half and
then add them to the bowl.

Peel the fresh litchis and remove the pits, or drain the cans of litchis.
Chop the litchis up coarsely.

Finally, cut the passion fruit in half and scoop out the seeds and pulp
into the bowl. Stir gently to combine.

Let the salad sit for at least 30 minutes before serving to let the flavors
mingle. This salad is best served at room temperature.

Ice Creams

Making a successful ice cream is more science than art, but these recipes give wonderfully soft and oh-so-smooth results that will leave everyone begging for more.

Chocolate Chip Ice Cream

MAKES ABOUT 4 CUPS

For the basic custard base
1 tablespoon agar powder (see page 186)
1⅔ cups rice milk
2 egg yolks
1⅔ cups heavy cream
½ oz raw lucuma powder (see page 186)
4 teaspoons raw organic local honey

For the chocolate flavoring
¼ cup unsweetened cocoa
2 teaspoons unsweetened vanilla extract
2 teaspoons stevia powder (see page 187)
2 oz no-added-sugar milk chocolate, chopped into small pieces

To make the basic custard base, stir the agar powder into the rice milk in a saucepan. Bring to a boil and cook until the agar powder has dissolved —about 5 minutes.

Beat the egg yolks with the cream, lucuma powder, and honey in a large bowl, then stir the hot rice milk into the mixture. Pour everything back into the pan and gently bring to a boil, stirring continuously so that the eggs don't curdle. When you begin to see bubbles rising to the surface, remove the pan from the heat.

Stir in the cocoa, vanilla extract, and stevia powder. Let the mixture cool completely, giving it a stir from time to time. When it is cold, stir in the chocolate pieces.

Pour the cooled mixture into your ice cream maker and churn according to the manufacturer's directions. If you don't have an ice cream maker, freeze the mixture in the bowl, then over the course of 2 hours, bring it out of the freezer every 30 minutes and blend it well in a food processor each time.

Transfer the ice cream to a 34 oz strong plastic tub with a lid, store in the freezer, and use within a week.

Vanilla Ice Cream

MAKES ABOUT 4 CUPS

1 quantity of basic custard base, as above

For the vanilla flavoring
5 teaspoons unsweetened vanilla extract
¼ teaspoon salt

To make the custard base, follow the first two steps as in the recipe above.

Stir in the vanilla extract and salt. Let the mixture cool completely. It will set as it cools, but don't worry—just give it a stir from time to time.

Follow the last two steps as in the recipe above.

Roasted bananas are the basis of this easy ice cream, giving a delicious sweetness that is offset perfectly by the salty chunks of peanut. For best results, let the ice cream defrost for 15 minutes before serving.

Banana & Salted Peanut Ice Cream

MAKES ABOUT 4 CUPS

6 bananas, about 1 lb 9 oz total weight
⅓ cup unsweetened crunchy peanut butter
½ cup heavy cream
½ cup salted peanuts, finely chopped

Preheat the oven to 400°F. Place the bananas in their skins in a roasting dish and bake for 20 minutes until blackened and soft.

Scrape out the banana flesh and juice into a bowl. Add the peanut butter and cream, and blend with an immersion blender for a few seconds until smooth. Let cool.

Transfer the mixture to an ice cream maker and churn according to the manufacturer's directions. If you don't have an ice cream maker, freeze the mixture in the bowl, then over the course of 2 hours, bring it out of the freezer every 30 minutes and blend it well in a food processor each time.

Stir in the peanuts, then transfer the ice cream to a 34 oz strong plastic tub with a lid, store in the freezer, and use within a week.

This ice cream gives a triple whammy of sensual delight: first you're seduced by the gorgeous pinky orange color, then just as you're tasting the creamy subtlety of the sweet papaya, you get the acid hit from the lime—terrific.

Papaya & Lime Ice Cream

MAKES ABOUT 3 CUPS

grated rind of 2 unwaxed limes
½ cup fresh lime juice
2 tablespoons stevia powder
    (see page 187)
2 tablespoons agar powder
    (see page 186)
1¼ cups heavy cream
2 ripe papayas, about 1 lb 7 oz
    total weight

Place the grated lime rind and juice, stevia powder, and agar powder in a saucepan and heat gently until the stevia and agar have almost dissolved. Pour in the cream and bring to a boil, then remove the pan from the heat.

Cut the papayas in half and scoop out the seeds with a spoon, then remove the skin with a vegetable peeler. Place the flesh in a blender and blend until smooth. Stir the papaya puree into the hot cream. Let the mixture cool completely.

Pour the cooled mixture into an ice cream maker and churn according to the manufacturer's directions. If you don't have an ice cream maker, freeze the mixture in the bowl, then over the course of 2 hours, bring it out of the freezer every 30 minutes and blend it well in a food processor each time.

Transfer the ice cream to a 25 oz strong plastic tub with a lid and store in the freezer. Try to eat the ice cream as soon as possible, as it will gradually become more and more icy. For best results, let the ice cream defrost for about 15 minutes before serving.

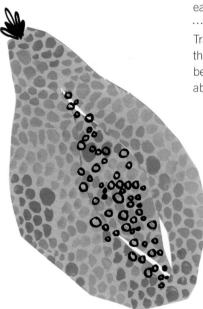

For a change from ice cream, this is a totally refreshing and summery frozen dessert, which is prepared as a solid block and then cut into slices to serve. For best results, use gorgeously ripe, juicy strawberries and eat within a couple of days of making it.

Strawberry Parfait

SERVES 8

sunflower oil, for oiling
scant 5 cups fresh strawberries
2 tablespoons agar powder (see page 186)
generous 2 cups heavy cream
½ teaspoon ground black pepper
1–2 teaspoons stevia powder (see page 187) or raw organic local honey (optional)

Line a 8¾ x 4½ x 3 inch/ 2 lb loaf pan with plastic wrap and then smear the plastic wrap with a thin layer of sunflower oil.

Hull the strawberries, then cut scant ¾ cup of them into thin slices about ⅛ inch thick. Line the pan with the strawberries slices—they should stick to the plastic wrap on the bottom and sides by themselves.

Stir the agar powder into the cream in a bowl until you can't see any powder left. Place the cream mixture with the remaining strawberries and the pepper in a blender or food processor and blend together. If your strawberries weren't very sweet, you could add the stevia powder or raw honey at this point to boost the flavor.

Pour the mixture into the loaf pan and freeze it for at least 4 hours. To serve, let defrost for 30 minutes. Turn the loaf pan upside down onto a serving plate and remove the pan to reveal your parfait, then peel off the plastic wrap. Cut into slices with a large sharp knife.

Kulfi is an Indian ice cream commonly made with condensed milk, almonds, and cardamom. I've used naturally sweet evaporated milk and pistachios instead. The nuttiness lends an irresistible texture. Though I've specified dariole molds, small plastic drinking glasses are a good alternative.

Pistachio Kulfi

SERVES 6

½ cup shelled unsalted pistachios
4 tablespoons water
1⅔ cups evaporated milk
½ cup whipping cream
1½ tablespoons stevia powder
    (see page 187)

Soak the pistachios in the measurement water for at least 4 hours or overnight.

Place the soaked nuts and any remaining water in a blender or food processor and add all the other ingredients. Blend for about 1 minute until the mixture has become a bit frothy and the texture is nearly smooth.

Line up 6 dariole molds and half-fill each one. Use a tablespoon to scoop out the rubbly nut mixture that will have collected at the bottom of the blender and distribute it evenly between the molds. Freeze for at least 4 hours until hardened.

To serve, sit the dariole molds in a flat-bottom bowl. Pour warm water into the bowl until it reaches just below the rim. After about 5 seconds, remove the molds and run a butter knife around the inside of each one. Turn the kulfi out onto serving plates. The chopped nut mixture will have colored the outside of the kulfi, giving an attractive, green and purple-speckled effect. Let soften for 5–10 minutes before serving.

At one point in my life I lived in Paris and fell in love with a litchi yogurt from my local store to the point of obsession. I have done my best to reincarnate it here, minus any added sugar, which thanks to the inherent sweetness of litchis isn't necessary anyway. This frozen yogurt is quick to make and best enjoyed semifreddo, as a dreamy mouthful of cool perfection.

Litchi Frozen Yogurt

MAKES ABOUT 3 CUPS

13 oz pitted fresh or drained canned litchis
1 cup whole Greek yogurt
pinch of salt

Place half the litchis in a food processor and process until smooth. Transfer to a bowl and stir in the yogurt and salt.

Finely dice the remaining litchis, add to the bowl, and stir together.

Ideally, you should now cover and leave the mixture in the refrigerator for an hour to let the sweetness and flavors develop, but if you're short of time, just skip this step.

Pour the mixture into a 25 oz strong plastic tub with a lid and freeze for 45 minutes. Use an electric whisk to blend everything thoroughly, then freeze for another 30 minutes. Whisk again. The frozen yogurt should now have the consistency of whipped cream and is ready to serve. Alternatively, keep it in the freezer until needed and let it defrost for 20 minutes, then whisk it with an electric whisk just before serving. The frozen yogurt will keep for up to a week.

Ginger is combined with the delicate flavor of melon in this refreshing, snowy-textured granita. Try it as a dessert in a decorative glass, topped with raspberries and balls of fresh melon.

Ginger Granita

MAKES ABOUT 4 CUPS

2 Galia melons, about 4 lb
   in total
6 teaspoons fresh lemon juice
½ teaspoon ground ginger

Quarter the melons and scrape out all the seeds. Use a tablespoon to scrape all the flesh out and place it in a blender with the lemon juice and ginger. Blend until just smooth.

Pour the mixture into a 34 oz strong plastic tub with a lid. Freeze for 2 hours, giving a quick stir every 30 minutes or so. After this time, blend everything again in the blender. You'll now have a much paler mixture with an even consistency.

Return to the tub and freeze for another 2 hours before serving. The granita needs to be consumed a couple of days after it is made or the texture will become too icy and hard.

The rum in this simple, dairy-free frozen dessert adds a bit of a kick and also helps keep the texture smooth. It's a great way to end a meal on a relaxed summer's day and I love its retro-kitsch vibe, especially when it's served with a cocktail umbrella and a slice of pineapple!

Piña Colada Ice

MAKES ABOUT 5 CUPS

2 (14 oz) cans pineapple chunks in juice
1¼ cups coconut cream (the liquid kind)
4 tablespoons white rum

Place all the ingredients in a food processor and process until well blended, then pour into a 50 oz strong plastic tub with a lid.

Freeze for 3 hours, then blend in the food processor again briefly. Return to the tub and refreeze for about 30 minutes or until needed. This is best eaten within 48 hours or the texture will become too hard.

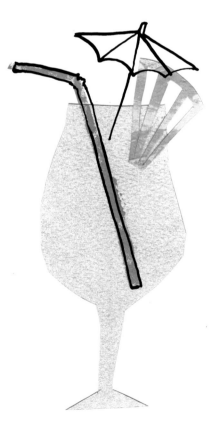

The smooth, intensely cold texture of real sorbet is unbeatable on a hot day and this recipe also has a hint of pepperiness, which gives an interesting contrast. Keeping sorbets silky is especially tricky when going sugar free because the sugar plays such an important role, but after experimenting a bit, I found a winning combination.

Orange & Star Anise Sorbet

MAKES ABOUT 2 CUPS

generous 2 cups fresh orange juice with bits
1 tablespoon agar powder (see page 186)
1 tablespoon stevia powder (see page 187)
2 star anise
large pinch of ground black pepper
2 egg whites

Pour the juice into a large saucepan. Stir in the agar powder, stevia powder, star anise, and black pepper and then simmer for 5 minutes or until the agar has dissolved. Transfer the liquid to a pitcher and discard the star anise.

Using an electric whisk, whisk the egg whites in a bowl until they form soft peaks. While continuing to whisk, very slowly pour in the hot juice in a thin stream, which will create a sort of cooked meringue. Don't worry if there seems to be liquid under the meringue. Chill the mixture in the refrigerator for an hour or so until completely cold.

Pour the chilled mixture into your ice cream maker and churn according to the manufacturer's directions. You can then transfer the sorbet to a 25 oz strong plastic tub with a lid and store in the freezer. It will become harder over time, so eat within a couple of days. Let soften for 5 minutes before serving.

Watermelon and evaporated milk is an amazingly tasty combination, while a touch of Campari adds an adults-only angle to these vibrant stripy ice pops—they're a firm favorite at beach or barbecue parties. Ice-pop molds vary quite a lot in their volume, but this should make enough for at least 6.

Campari & Watermelon Pops

MAKES ABOUT 2 CUPS

10 oz peeled and seeded watermelon
1 tablespoon Campari
generous ¾ cup evaporated milk

Place the watermelon flesh in a blender or food processor and blend until smooth. Stir in the Campari.

To create the stripes, first pour the watermelon mixture into your ice pop molds to fill each by one-third. Freeze for an hour.

Now pour in evaporated milk to fill another one-third of your molds. Attach foil to the top of each mold with an elastic band, then insert a ice pop stick through the foil into the evaporated milk layer. Freeze for aanother 45 minutes–1 hour until reasonably firm.

Remove the foil and top off with watermelon mixture, leaving a space at the top of the mold to allow for the expansion of the ice. Pop the ice pops back in the freezer. They will be fully hardened after about 3 hours. The ice pops are best served within a week.

Everyday Snacks

I love the windmill shape of these pretty Danish pastries. Keeping the skin on the apples not only makes them healthier but also gives the twists a more colorful look.

Cream Cheese & Apple Twists

MAKES 8

all-purpose flour, for dusting
8 oz ready-made puff pastry
2 dessert apples, cored and
  chopped into small pieces,
  skin left on
3 teaspoons water
scant ¼ cup cream cheese
1 egg, beaten

Preheat the oven to 400°F. Sprinkle a little flour across a baking sheet.

Place the chopped apple in a small saucepan with the measurement water and heat gently for about 5 minutes until softened.

Roll out the pastry on a counter well dusted with flour to a rectangle about 14 x 7 inches, and about ⅛ inch thick. Cut into 8 pastry squares. On each square, make a cut from each corner toward the center using a sharp knife, stopping about halfway in.

Spread the cream cheese across the center of each square and then distribute the apple on top of each portion of cream cheese.

To make the twist shape, bring the left-hand side of each corner into the center. Secure the tips in place by brushing with the beaten egg, pressing together and sticking a toothpick through the middle. Repeat for the other pastries. Brush a little beaten egg across all visible pastry surfaces.

Transfer to the floured baking sheet and bake for 20 minutes until golden. Remove the toothpicks. These pastries are best served warm.

These snack bars are ready in minutes and make a filling midmorning pick-me-up that should prevent you diving into the cookie jar. Figs, nuts, and seeds give texture and taste—simple but totally moreish.

Peanut Snack Bars

MAKES 12

7 oz soft dried figs
scant ½ cup unsweetened crunchy
   peanut butter
¼ cup sunflower seeds
⅓ cup pumpkin seeds
⅓ cup whole-wheat
   all-purpose flour
2 tablespoons sunflower oil
2 teaspoons water

Remove the tough stalky part at the top of each fig. Place the figs in a food processor, add all the other ingredients, and pulse until you have a mixture with the texture of fine crumbs. Press the crumbs firmly together to form a dough.

Roll out the dough on a counter to a thickness of about ½ inch—a rectangle about 7 x 6 inches is perfect. If there are cracks, press the dough more firmly. Cut into 12 slices. Store in the refrigerator and eat within 7 days.

These bars are made from dense German-style rye bread—the kind that usually comes in a square block, presliced. Rye bread is already packed full of nutrients and here I've added prunes, pumpkin seeds, and semisweet chocolate to create a pleasingly portable snack for people on the go.

Chocolate & Rye Energy Bars

MAKES 8

sunflower oil, for oiling
4 tablespoons milk
1 egg
8 oz German-style rye bread
3½ oz pitted prunes
3½ oz no-added-sugar semisweet chocolate
⅓ cup pumpkin seeds

Preheat the oven to 350°F. Lightly oil an 8¾ x 4½ x 3 inch/2 lb loaf pan with a little sunflower oil.

Whisk the milk and egg together in a large bowl. Crumble in the rye bread in smallish pieces. Give the mixture a stir, then let sit for about 10 minutes.

Finely chop the prunes and half the chocolate, then stir both into the rye mixture along with the pumpkin seeds.

Break the remaining chocolate into small pieces. Place in a heatproof bowl set over a saucepan of barely simmering water (make sure the bottom of the bowl doesn't touch the water), or in the microwave on a medium setting for about 45 seconds (my preferred method), until nearly all the chocolate has melted. Give it a stir and let rest for a couple of minutes until it has all melted. Stir the melted chocolate into the rye mixture.

Transfer the mixture to the loaf pan and smooth the top with a spatula. Bake for 20 minutes.

Let cool, then cut into slices. The bars will keep for up to a week in the refrigerator.

This is a fabulous, fudgy gingerbread made only with raw ingredients, so as well as being rammed full of goodness it takes just moments to make. It'll keep for up to 3 days in the refrigerator.

Raw Gingerbread

MAKES 12 PIECES

6½ oz pitted dried dates
½ cup raw cashew nuts
⅔ cup finely shredded carrot
scant ⅔ cup whole-wheat all-
   purpose flour
grated rind of 1 unwaxed orange
1 tablespoon sunflower oil
1 teaspoon ground ginger
1 teaspoon ground cinnamon
2 tablespoons slivered almonds

Place all the ingredients except the slivered almonds in a food processor and process for a minute or so until everything comes together in a doughy lump. Stir in the slivered almonds.

Use a spatula to scrape everything out and then pat the mixture into a square about 1 inch thick. Cut into 12 pieces and transfer to a plastic tub with a lid. Chill in the refrigerator for 4 hours, or overnight, until the gingerbread has firmed to the texture of fudge.

Variation

You can make a gluten-free version of the gingerbread by replacing the whole-wheat flour with a gluten-free flour blend.

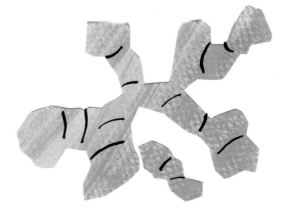

This banana bread makes a nutritious snack: it's packed with bananas, which are rich in manganese and potassium, and the whole-wheat flour and sunflower seeds contribute extra goodness in the form of fiber and vitamins B and E. It's great just as it is, or with butter or even a slice of cheese.

Banana Bread

MAKES ABOUT 12 SLICES

4 ripe bananas, about 1 lb 7 oz
5 tablespoons unsalted butter, melted, plus extra for greasing
1 egg, beaten
1¼ cups white all-purpose flour
scant ½ cup whole-wheat all-purpose flour
4 teaspoons baking powder
½ teaspoon salt
½ cup sunflower seeds

Preheat the oven to 400°F. Lightly grease a 8¾ x 4½ x 3 inch/2 lb loaf pan with a little butter.

Peel and mash the bananas in a large bowl (a few lumps are OK). Add the melted butter, followed by the egg, and stir well.

Add both flours, the baking powder, and salt to the bowl. Gently fold everything together until well mixed. Set aside about 1 tablespoon of the sunflower seeds, then fold the rest into the mixture.

Use a spatula to transfer the mixture to the loaf pan. Shake gently to distribute it evenly in the pan and then smooth the top with the spatula. Sprinkle the reserved sunflower seeds on top.

Bake for 55–65 minutes until well browned and risen. Let cool in the pan.

Variation

You can make the banana bread dairy free by using dairy-free margarine in place of the butter. Make it vegan as well by omitting the egg and adding 4 tablespoons soy milk instead.

These waffles make a great choice to start your day—eaten with berries, they are a source of all the major food groups. I love them like this, with their hint of fragrant cardamom and a little sweetness from the rice milk.

Cardamom Waffles with Berries

SERVES 4

3½ tablespoons unsalted butter, melted, plus extra for greasing

1¼ cups whole-wheat all-purpose flour

1¼ cups white all-purpose flour

1 teaspoon baking powder

4 eggs, beaten

1¾ cups rice milk

1 green cardamom pod

1 cup fresh blueberries

1 cup fresh strawberries, hulled and halved

scant 1¼ cups fresh raspberries

Pour the melted butter into a bowl and stir in both flours, the baking powder, eggs, and half the rice milk to form a smooth paste. Gradually beat in the remaining rice milk.

Break open the cardamom pod and remove the seeds. Crush them with the back of a teaspoon, then sprinkle them into the batter by rubbing them between your fingers and thumb so that they crumble to dust. Stir in.

Preheat your waffle iron to medium-high and lightly grease with a little butter. Pour in the first portion of batter and cook for 4–5 minutes until the waffle is browned and crispy. Repeat the process until the batter is used up. If necessary, the cooked waffles can be kept warm in a low oven while the others are cooking.

Serve the waffles warm, sprinkled with the fresh berries.

These buns make the perfect project for a happy afternoon in the kitchen, mooching about and not doing anything too strenuous. The cinnamon-laced scent as the buns cook is totally uplifting too.

Swedish Cherry Buns

MAKES 12

For the dough
1 dessert apple, about 5 oz
1 green cardamom pod
scant 2¼ cups strong white flour, plus extra for dusting
generous ½ cup whole-wheat all-purpose flour
1 (¼ oz) sachet active dry yeast
generous ¾ cup milk, plus a little extra if needed
1 egg
½ teaspoon salt

For the filling
2 tablespoons unsalted butter, very soft
2 teaspoons ground cinnamon
generous ¼ cup soft dried apricots
scant ½ cup dried cherries

For the topping
2 tablespoons milk
scant ¼ cup shelled unsalted pistachios, finely chopped

To make the dough, cut the apple in half and set one half aside, cut side down, for the filling. Core and coarsely shred the other half (leave the skin on), then place in a large bowl. Break open the cardamom pod and remove the seeds. Crush them to a powder using the back of a teaspoon and add to the bowl with all the remaining dough ingredients. Stir well, then knead the mixture to bring it together into a dough—add a little more milk or flour, if necessary.

Knead the dough by hand on a counter lightly dusted with flour for another 5 minutes or using a freestanding electric mixer fitted with the dough hook.

Roll out the dough on the floured counter to a 10¼ inch square, about ¼ inch thick.

Now make the filling. Beat the butter and cinnamon together and spread across the dough, taking care to make an even layer that reaches every edge. Core and coarsely shred the reserved apple half (again, leave the skin on), and chop the apricots very finely, then stir them both together with the cherries. Distribute the mixture on top of the butter.

Roll the dough into a cylinder shape and cut into 12 slices. Place each slice facing upward in a paper muffin liner. Leave the muffin pan somewhere warm for 1–2 hours until the dough has at least doubled in size and filled the paper liners.

Preheat the oven to 425°F. Brush each bun with a little of the milk and sprinkle with the pistachios. Bake for 12–15 minutes until the buns are golden. Serve warm or cold; they will keep surprisingly well for a couple of days (warm them before serving).

This is a seriously versatile loaf—serve it warm from the oven as a fragrant and welcoming treat when friends come around, eat it toasted and buttered for breakfast, or just enjoy it with a slice of cheese as a nutritious snack.

Fruit Braid

MAKES ABOUT 15 SLICES

2 cups strong white flour, plus extra
    for dusting
scant ⅔ cup whole-wheat all-
    purpose flour
2 teaspoons active dry yeast
1½ teaspoons ground mixed spice
pinch of salt
1 large unwaxed orange, about 8 oz
1 teaspoon sunflower oil, plus extra
    for oiling
¼ cup golden raisins
scant ¼ cup sunflower seeds
1 tablespoon milk

Lightly oil a baking sheet with a little sunflower oil.

Place the both flours in a bowl with the yeast, mixed spice, and salt. Grate in the rind of the orange and then give everything a stir.

Juice the orange and scrape out all the nice juicy bits (avoiding the bitter white pith) into a measuring cup and make up to 1 cup with warm water.

Pour the liquid into the flour mixture and add the oil. Stir together as far as possible, then get your hands in and knead the mixture to a lovely soft and aromatic dough.

Knead the dough for 3–4 minutes on a counter well dusted with flour. It should be really soft but not sticky—add a little extra flour if necessary. Knead in the golden raisins and sunflower seeds.

Cut the dough into 3 equal-size pieces. Roll each one into a sausage shape about 14 inches long, tapered at both ends.

Braid the 3 sausage shapes together and pinch the ends to a point. Place the loaf on the baking sheet, then brush the milk across the top of the braid. Leave for 1–2 hours in a warm place until doubled in size.

Preheat the oven to 425°F. Bake the loaf for 20 minutes until golden brown. Enjoy hot or cold.

Variation

For a vegan/dairy-free version of this recipe, use soy milk in place of the cows' milk.

In this oatmeal, the oats are left to soak in order for them to soften and for the flavors to mingle. Don't be put off by the extra time involved because making it is easily slotted into a morning routine—I like to do the preparation, go off and have a shower, and then heat it and eat it. So simple!

Apple Oatmeal

SERVES 2

½ cup rolled oats
1¼ cups water
1 large dessert apple, about 7 oz,
   cored and coarsely shredded
   (leave the skin on)
2 tablespoons plain yogurt
1 tablespoon slivered Brazil nuts

Mix the oats, measurement water, and shredded apple together in a saucepan. Let soak for about 10 minutes, then simmer the mixture for 4–5 minutes until thickened and slightly translucent.

Spoon out the oatmeal into 2 bowls. Add a tablespoonful of yogurt to the top of each, then sprinkle the slivered Brazil nuts over the top and serve.

Variations

For a dairy-free breakfast, use soy yogurt. Use gluten-free oats for a gluten-free version of this recipe.

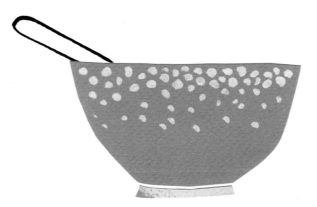

This is my perfect muesli—not too sweet, by turns crunchy and chewy, and with a great selection of nuts, seeds, and fruit that means I can bask in the glow of racking up several of my 5-a-day by 8 a.m. Try it with plain Greek yogurt or with fresh milk.

Mango & Cranberry Muesli

MAKES ABOUT 15 SERVINGS

4 oz rye or whole-wheat flakes
1 teaspoon sunflower oil
½ teaspoon ground cinnamon
⅓ cup pumpkin seeds
⅓ cup flaked coconut
¼ cup slivered almonds
2⅓ cups rolled oats
2 oz dried unsweetened mango, finely chopped
⅓ cup dried unsweetened cranberries
scant ¼ cup shelled raw pistachios

Preheat the oven to 350°F. Get out 2 baking sheets. Spread your rye or wheat flakes out on 1 baking sheet.

Stir the oil and cinnamon together in a bowl. Tip in the pumpkin seeds, coconut, and almonds and stir until evenly coated in the oil and cinnamon mixture. Spread the mixture onto the second baking sheet. Place both baking sheets in the oven. After 10 minutes, remove the nut mixture but leave the rye/wheat flakes for another 5 minutes to get nicely crisp. Let everything cool completely.

Place the oats in a 34 oz clip-top jar. Add the mango, cranberries, and pistachios. Finally, pour in the rye/wheat flakes and the toasted nut mixture. Give everything a stir and a shake and clip the lid shut. The muesli should keep well for a couple of weeks.

Variation

I've used unsweetened cranberries here, but they are a little tart. You can substitute them with raisins if you prefer a sweeter muesli.

These grissini cost a fraction of the artisanal ones from your local deli, but their delicate forms and sprinkling of poppy seeds mean they look and taste just as good. Try them dipped into hummus or a spicy salsa.

Poppy Seed Grissini

MAKES ABOUT 50

½ cup warm water
1 teaspoon active dry yeast
1 teaspoon good-quality fresh apple juice
1 cup strong white flour, plus extra for dusting
2 tablespoons whole-wheat all-purpose flour
¼ teaspoon fine salt
2 tablespoons olive oil, plus extra for oiling
1 teaspoon milk
1 tablespoon poppy seeds

Lightly oil a couple of baking sheets.

Stir together the measurement warm water, yeast, and apple juice in a bowl.

Place both flours and salt in a large bowl. Pour in the yeast liquid and the oil, mix it in, and bring together into a dough.

Knead for a good couple of minutes on a counter well dusted with flour until you have a soft and supple dough—add a little extra flour if it seems too sticky.

Roll out the dough on the floured counter to a rectangle about 8 x 10 inches, and about ¼ inch thick. Brush the top with the milk and then sprinkle over the poppy seeds.

Using a ruler and a pizza cutter, cut the rectangle along the long sides into 25 strips about ½ inch wide.

Pick up a strip and gently stretch it so that it is roughly double its length (though don't let the strip get too thin in any one spot or it will overcook later on). Break it in half and twist each half 2 or 3 times before placing it on the baking sheet. Repeat for the remaining strips.

Let the strips rise for about an hour in a warm place until they have roughly doubled in thickness.

Preheat the oven to 400°F. Bake the grissini for 15 minutes, then reduce the oven temperature to 275°F for another 5–10 minutes until they are golden brown and hard all the way through. Let them cool on a wire rack, then store them in a tall airtight jar.

Variation

Use soy milk in place of the milk if you want a dairy-free recipe.

These scones are a favorite snack of my niece Cecily—she loves the crunchy, cheesy crust and fluffy center. They are lovely cold, but even better slightly warm from the oven and spread with butter or eaten just as they are.

Smoked Cheese & Apple Scones

MAKES 6

1 dessert apple, about 5 oz
3½ oz Bavarian smoked cheese
scant ⅔ cup whole-wheat all-purpose flour
scant ⅔ cup white all-purpose flour, plus extra for dusting
2½ teaspoons baking powder
1 tablespoon sunflower oil, plus extra for oiling
1 egg, beaten
2 teaspoons milk
1 tablespoon sunflower seeds

Preheat the oven to 425°F. Lightly oil a baking sheet with sunflower oil.

Shred each side of the apple in turn against a box grater until you reach the core, working around the apple until all the flesh has been shredded, then discard the core. Place the shredded apple in a bowl. Next, shred the cheese and add to the bowl, then add both flours, the baking powder, and oil.

Add the egg and stir everything together to create a soft and somewhat sticky dough.

Dust a counter lightly with flour and flatten the dough to a thickness of about 1¼ inches. Use a 2½ inch round cookie cutter to cut out your scones, gathering together the trimmings as necessary, until you have used up all the dough—you should get 6, but it does depend on the exact thickness of the dough. Place them on the baking sheet and then brush them with the milk and sprinkle the sunflower seeds on top.

Bake the scones for 15 minutes until risen and browned. They will spread a little as they cook. Let cool on a wire rack.

Inspired by the good old chicken korma, this tasty blend of spicy cashews, almonds, and pumpkin seeds mixed with flaked coconut and pieces of dried mango will liven up any hike.

Spiced Trail Mix

MAKES 14 OZ

1 cup raw cashew nuts
scant 1 cup whole almonds
scant ⅔ cup pumpkin seeds
2 teaspoons sunflower oil
1 tablespoon garam masala
2 oz dried unsweetened mango,
    finely chopped
1 oz flaked coconut salt

Place the cashews, almonds, and seeds in a large skillet over medium-high heat. Dry-fry for about 10 minutes, stirring occasionally, until the nuts have started to brown and the pumpkin seeds start to pop.

Remove the pan from the heat. Mix the oil and garam masala together, then add to the pan and quickly give everything a good stir. Add salt to taste and then let everything cool completely.

Place the mango in an airtight jar, add the coconut and cooled nut mixture, and give the jar a shake—your spicy snack is ready to go.

Pumpkin seeds are fantastically nutritious, but can be uninspiring eaten raw. After a rapid roasting and a super-tasty umami coating, they turn into the queen of snacks.

Pumpkin Pops

MAKES 10 OZ

1 teaspoon light soy sauce
2 teaspoons water
2½ cups pumpkin seeds

Preheat the oven to 400°F.

Mix the soy sauce and measurement water together in a large bowl. Pour in the pumpkin seeds and stir until they are lightly coated in the soy mixture.

Spread the seeds out on a baking sheet and place it in the oven. After about 8 minutes you'll hear slight popping noises coming from the oven as the seeds expand. Remove them from the oven after 10–12 minutes, when the majority of the seeds will have swelled and the coating has dried.

Let cool completely, then store in an airtight jar and eat within a week.

For Children

These cheese-flavored, milk-enriched breadsticks taste great by themselves or dipped into a little hummus. The kids love making the supple dough, providing a fun activity for an afternoon as well as a snack.

Cheesy Breadsticks

MAKES 16

1 cup strong white flour, plus extra for dusting

1¼ cups whole-wheat all-purpose flour

2 teaspoons active dry yeast

1 teaspoon olive oil, plus extra for oiling

1 teaspoon mustard

1 cup warm milk, plus extra for brushing

generous ¾ cup shredded cheddar cheese or other hard cheese

¼ cup brown flaxseeds

Lightly oil a couple of baking sheets with a little olive oil.

Place both flours, the yeast, oil, and mustard in a bowl. Pour in the warm milk and knead the mixture until it comes together as a soft dough.

Knead in the cheese, then continue kneading on a counter well dusted with flour for a minute, adding a little extra flour if it feels too sticky—the dough should be very soft, but shouldn't stick to your fingers.

Cut the dough into 16 equal-size pieces, then roll and stretch each one to form a breadstick about 10 inches long. Brush the tops of the breadsticks with some warm milk. Pour the flaxseeds onto a large plate and roll each breadstick in the seeds before placing them on the baking sheets.

Let the breadsticks rise for an hour in a warm place until roughly doubled in size.

Preheat the oven to 425°F. Bake the breadsticks for 10 minutes. Let cool on a wire rack.

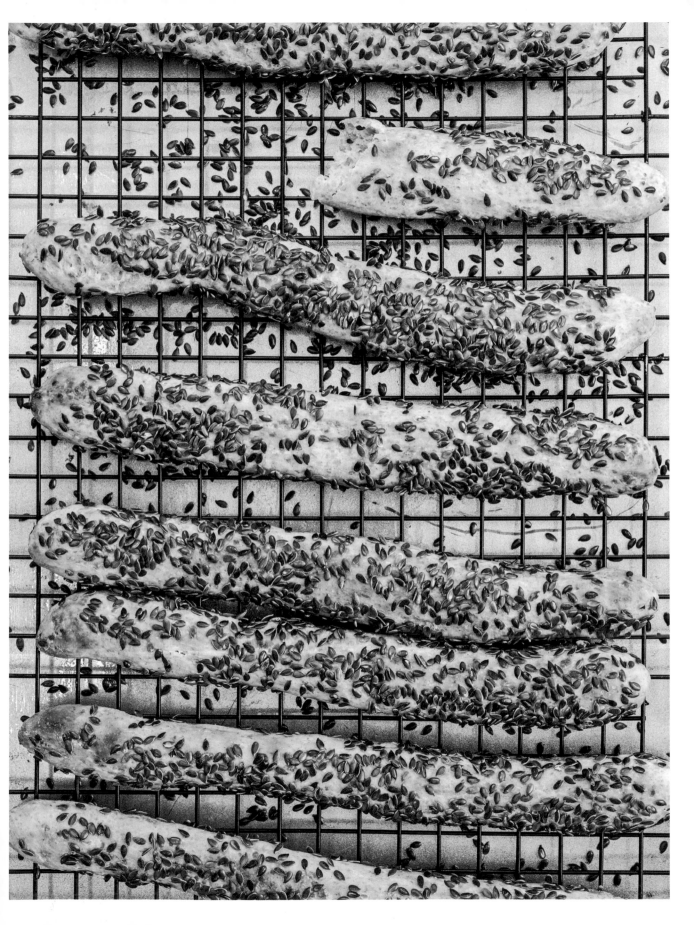

My children are always complaining that they are hungry, but it's hard to keep their hands out of the cookie jar. If that sounds familiar, then try offering these tomato and herb spirals warm from the oven as a tempting alternative to sugary snacks.

Tomato & Herb Spirals

MAKES 8

For the dough
sunflower oil, for oiling
2 teaspoons active dry yeast
1 cup hand-hot water
1 tablespoon tomato paste
scant 2¼ cups strong white flour,
   plus extra for dusting
scant ⅔ cup whole-wheat all-
   purpose flour
pinch of salt

For the filling
3 oz cooked carrot
3 tablespoons tomato paste
3 tablespoons milk
½ teaspoon dried oregano
scant ½ cup shredded cheddar
   cheese or other hard cheese

Lightly oil a 10 x 6¼ inch baking dish with a little sunflower oil.

To make the dough, stir the yeast, measurement hand-hot water, and tomato paste together in a small bowl. Place both flours in a bowl with the salt. Stir in the liquid, then knead the mixture to bring it together into a dough.

Knead by hand on a counter lightly dusted with flour for another couple of minutes or using a freestanding electric mixer fitted with the dough hook.

Roll out the dough on the floured counter into a 10¼ inch square, about ¼ inch thick.

Now make the filling. Place the cooked carrot, tomato paste, milk, and oregano in a food processor or blender and process until smooth. Spread the mixture across the top of the dough.

Roll the dough into a cylinder and cut into 8 equal-size slices. Place each slice facing upward in the baking dish. Leave somewhere warm for 1–2 hours until the dough has more than doubled in size and the spirals have completely filled the dish. Sprinkle with the shredded cheese.

Preheat the oven to 425°F. Bake the spirals for 12–15 minutes until they are golden and all the dough is cooked. Serve warm or cold.

Dates and roasted butternut squash help to provide the all-important "squidge" factor in these brownies and also offer a great way to give kids extra nutrients.

Chocolate Brownies

MAKES 16

sunflower oil, for oiling
7 oz butternut squash
7 tablespoons unsalted butter, chopped
2 teaspoons stevia powder (see page 187)
3 oz no-added-sugar semisweet chocolate, broken into pieces
3 eggs
3½ oz pitted dried dates
scant ½ cup whole-wheat flour
scant ½ cup all-purpose flour
1 teaspoon baking powder
pinch of salt
½ cup walnuts, chopped

Variation

Use dairy-free margarine in place of butter for a dairy-free version of this recipe.

Preheat the oven to 400°F. Lightly oil an 8 inch square baking pan with sunflower oil, or line the pan with parchment paper.

Seed the butternut squash and chop into pieces about 1 inch square. You can keep the skin on—it provides extra nutrients and you'll never notice it in the finished brownies. Spread the chopped squash out in the baking pan and roast for 20 minutes until soft. Let cool for about 10 minutes.

Meanwhile, place the butter, stevia powder, and chocolate in a saucepan over low heat, stirring occasionally. As soon as most of it has melted, remove the pan from the heat. Let stand until everything has melted.

Place the roasted squash, eggs, and dates in a food processor and process for about 1 minute until the mixture is as smooth as possible. Now add both flours, the baking powder, and salt, followed by the melted chocolate mixture. Process for about 30 seconds until everything is really well combined. Stir in the walnuts.

Spread the batter across the baking pan and smooth it flat with a spatula. Bake for 12–15 minutes until the brownie has shrunk away from the sides of the pan but is still squidgy in the middle. Let cool in the pan, then cut into 16 pieces.

This recipe uses basic science to fascinating effect—magic color-changing pancakes, packed with goodness, all thanks to shredded beet and a few common ingredients. It's the perfect treat for budding chemists everywhere. Watch how the lusciously pink batter darkens or lightens, then see more magic happen in the pan. If only all cooking was so dramatic!

Magic Pancakes

SERVES 4

1¼ cups all-purpose flour
scant ½ cup whole-wheat
   all-purpose flour
1 egg
½ cup milk
2 tablespoons sunflower oil, plus
   extra for frying
3 oz finely shredded fresh beet
4 tablespoons sour cream, plus
   extra (optional) to serve
1 teaspoon baking powder
1 teaspoon baking soda
1½ cups fresh blueberries
cooked bacon, to serve (optional)

Place both flours in a bowl. Stir in the egg, milk, and oil until you have a smooth batter. Add the shredded beet to create a lovely pink color.

Now transfer half the batter to a different bowl. To the first bowl add the sour cream and baking powder. The batter will become marginally more pinky red.

To the second bowl add the baking soda. After a few minutes, you'll notice the color darken to a purply pink.

Divide the blueberries evenly between the 2 batters and stir them in.

Heat a large skillet over medium heat and smear with a little sunflower oil. Use a tablespoon to add dollops of batter to the pan–depending on the size of your pan, you might fit 3 or 4 dollops on at a time. You'll see bubbles popping on the surface. After 1–2 minutes, when the bubbles ease off and the pancakes lose their gloss, flip them over and fry for another minute or so until browned.

The baking soda pancakes will change from purple to yellow, while the baking powder pancakes will still be a violent pink. Enjoy them warm, with extra sour cream and bacon, if desired.

Variation

You could make this recipe dairy free by using soy milk and soy yogurt in place of the cows' milk and sour cream.

These simple raw flapjacks are made almost entirely of oats, nuts, and fruit, yet they combine to create a moreish snack. The fact they are frozen makes them especially appealing to kids.

Apple Freezer Flapjacks

MAKES 10

sunflower oil, for oiling
1¾ cups rolled oats
3½ tablespoons unsweetened smooth cashew nut butter
¼ cup seedless raisins
2 tablespoons unsalted butter
1 large dessert apple, about 7 oz

Variation

Use gluten-free oats for a gluten-free version of this recipe.

Lightly oil a 8¾ x 4½ x 3 inch/2 lb loaf pan with a little sunflower oil.

Put the oats in a food processor and pulse 3 or 4 times until you have a textured powder. Add the cashew nut butter, raisins, and butter, then continue pulsing until the mixture is even in texture and the raisins have been thoroughly chopped up. Remove roughly half the mixture and set aside.

Coarsely shred each side of the apple in turn against a box grater until you reach the core, working around the apple until all the flesh has been shredded, then discard the core. Add the shredded apple to the food processor and blend it with the remaining oat mixture for 4–5 seconds until smooth. Stir in the reserved oat mixture.

Scoop the mixture into the loaf pan and smooth down the top with the back of a spoon. Use a sharp knife to cut the mixture into 10 pieces. Freeze for at least an hour in a strong plastic tub with a lid (they'll keep for up to a week like this), then defrost for 10 minutes before eating.

This quick and easy chocolate treat requires no cooking and offers a nutritious mixture of dried fruit, nuts, and seeds, all encased in a buttery chocolate mass. I've used whole-wheat crackers to give an element of cookie texture, but if you want something with no added salt, use sugar-free baby rusks instead.

Chocolate Refrigerator Cake

MAKES 8 SLICES

sunflower oil, for greasing
3½ oz no-added-sugar milk chocolate, broken into pieces
3½ tablespoons unsalted butter, chopped
generous ¼ cup dried apricots, finely chopped
2 oz unsweetened whole-wheat crackers, crushed
generous ¼ cup dry unsweetened coconut
¼ cup slivered almonds
2 tablespoons pumpkin seeds

Lightly oil an 8¾ x 4½ x 3 inch/2 lb loaf pan with a little sunflower oil.

Place the chocolate and butter in a saucepan over low heat, stirring occasionally. As soon as most of it has melted, remove the pan from the heat and let stand until everything has melted.

Stir all the other ingredients into the melted chocolate mixture until everything is thoroughly combined.

Transfer the mixture to the loaf pan and press it down firmly with the back of a metal tablespoon to compact it and flatten the surface. Chill in the refrigerator for 30 minutes.

Run a blunt knife between the edge of the pan and the cake to extract it from the pan and then slice it into 8 pieces with a sharp knife. Store in an airtight container in the refrigerator for up to 3 days.

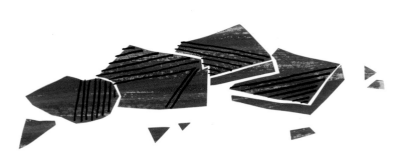

These sticky buns are made from the same kind of enriched dough as doughnuts but are baked rather than fried so they contain less fat—and little hands can help with the whole process. These are lovely eaten warm.

Sticky Doughnut Buns

MAKES 10

1 tablespoon sunflower oil, plus extra for oiling
generous ⅓ cup warm milk
1 teaspoon active dry yeast
1 teaspoon good-quality fresh apple juice
1 teaspoon stevia powder (see page 187)
scant 1⅔ cups strong white flour, plus extra for dusting
¼ teaspoon ground nutmeg
2 tablespoons unsalted butter, melted
1 egg, beaten
2 teaspoons raw organic local honey, warmed
½ teaspoon ground cinnamon

Lightly oil a baking sheet with a little sunflower oil.

Stir the milk and yeast together with the stevia powder and apple juice in a small bowl. Mix the flour and nutmeg together in a bowl. Pour in the milk mixture, then stir in the melted butter and egg. Knead the mixture to bring it together into a dough.

Knead by hand on a counter lightly dusted with flour for another couple of minutes or using a freestanding electric mixer fitted with the dough hook until you have a soft and supple dough. You may need a little extra flour—the dough shouldn't be sticky.

Divide the dough into 10 equal-size pieces and roll each one into a ball. Space them out evenly on the baking sheet and cover with a damp dish towel. Leave somewhere warm for an hour or so until they have doubled in volume.

Preheat the oven to 400°F. Brush the tops of the buns with the warmed honey and then bake for 12–15 minutes until they are a rich golden brown color and sound hollow when tapped on the bottom.

Sprinkle the warm buns with the cinnamon and serve.

Variation

Add ¼ cup raisins to the dough if you want a fruited bun.

These soft cookie stars make a good low-sugar finger food for toddlers and don't contain any added salt. A little whole-wheat flour (and raw lucuma powder if you have some—see page 186) adds fiber and nutrients.

Ginger Stars

MAKES ABOUT 20

generous ¾ cup white all-purpose
   flour, plus extra for dusting
scant ½ cup whole-wheat flour
5 tablespoons unsalted butter,
   chilled and cut into chunks,
   plus extra for greasing
1 tablespoon raw lucuma powder
   (see page 186, optional)
1½ teaspoons ground ginger
1 teaspoon baking powder
1 small ripe banana, about 3¾ oz,
   peeled and mashed
1 tablespoon milk
¼ cup raisins

Preheat the oven to 400°F. Lightly grease a couple of baking sheets with a little butter.

Mix both flours together in a bowl, add the butter, and rub in with your fingertips until the mixture resembles bread crumbs (you can pulse the ingredients in a food processor instead, if you prefer).

Stir in the lucuma powder, if using, ginger, baking powder, and mashed banana. Knead everything together into a soft dough. If it seems sticky, add a little more flour.

Roll out the dough on a counter dusted with flour to a thickness of ¼ inch. Use a 2½ inch star cookie cutter to cut out star shapes, rerolling the trimmings as necessary, until you have used up all the dough. Place the stars on the baking sheets.

Brush the stars with the milk. Decorate with the raisins, pushing them firmly into position. Bake the stars for 10–12 minutes until they are risen, slightly browned and cooked all the way through. Let them cool on a wire rack.

Crunchy cornflake cakes are a perennial favorite with children, but instead of loading these with syrup I have used peanut butter as a base. This means they are not only far lower in sugar but also higher in nutrients—peanuts are a great source of protein and vitamin E.

Crispy Cakes

MAKES 12

3 tablespoons unsalted butter, cut into chunks
½ cup unsweetened crunchy peanut butter
3 tablespoons dried milk powder
1½ tablespoons unsweetened cocoa
1 tablespoon raw organic local honey
2 cups unsweetened cornflakes
⅓ cup raisins

Line a 12-section cupcake pan with paper cupcake liners.

Place the butter, peanut butter, milk powder, cocoa, and honey in a saucepan over low heat until the butter has melted. Stir until everything has combined.

Stir in the cornflakes and raisins.

Divide the cornflake mixture between the paper cupcake liners. Chill in the refrigerator for about 30 minutes until the crispy cakes have set. They are best eaten the same day.

These little semicircular parcels are made from a yeast dough, but what makes them unusual is the fact that they are fried, not baked. This is because this recipe is based on one from the Middle Ages where oven baking was a rarity. The benefits are not only speed and a lovely buttery crust but also that they can be easily cooked over an open fire— which made them an instant hit with my children!

Apple & Blackberry Parcels

MAKES 6 OR 8

For the dough
½ dessert apple, about 3 oz
generous ¾ cup all-purpose flour
generous ¾ cup whole-wheat
   all-purpose flour
1 (¼oz) sachet active dry yeast
¾ cup warm milk
pinch of salt
7 tablespoons unsalted butter

For the filling
2½ dessert apples, about 12 oz
   total weight
scant ¼ cup whole hazelnuts,
   coarsely chopped
½ cup fresh blackberries
½ teaspoon ground cinnamon

Core and coarsely shred the apple half (leave the skin on), then place in a large bowl. Add both flours, the yeast, warm milk, and salt and knead everything together into a soft dough (you may need to add a little extra flour if it feels sticky). Cover the bowl with a clean dish towel and leave somewhere warm for an hour or so until the dough has doubled in volume.

Meanwhile, for the filling, coarsely shred each side of the apples in turn against a box grater until you reach the core, working around each apple until all the flesh has been shredded. Discard the core. Mix the shredded apple with the hazelnuts in a bowl, then stir in the blackberries and cinnamon.

Divide the dough into 6 or 8 equal-size portions (depending on the size of your skillet). Flatten each one into a circle about ¼ inch thick. Lightly moisten the outer edges with a drop of water. Place a dollop of filling on one side of each circle and then fold the circle in half, sealing it closed by pressing the edges together with a fork.

Heat a skillet over medium heat and add a generous amount of butter. Fry the parcels for about 3–5 minutes on each side until crispy and golden brown.

Variation

Omit the hazelnuts if you want a nut-free recipe. If you want a dairy-free or vegan recipe, use dairy-free margarine in place of butter and soy milk in place of cows' milk.

You can enjoy these fritters just as they are, or for a sweeter treat, drizzle a little maple syrup over the top just before serving. Although I've used pineapple, sliced banana works well too.

Pineapple Fritters

MAKES ABOUT 8

scant ½ cup white all-purpose flour
2 tablespoons whole-wheat all-purpose flour
4 tablespoons milk
1 egg, beaten
1 (14 oz) can pineapple rings in juice, drained and juice set aside
sunflower oil, for frying

Note

This recipe uses very hot oil, so don't allow children near the saucepan and don't leave it unattended at any time.

Mix both flours, the milk, and egg with 2 tablespoons of the pineapple juice in a bowl until you have a batter with the consistency of Greek yogurt.

Pat the pineapple rings dry with paper towels.

Let the batter stand while you fill a heavy saucepan with sunflower oil to a depth of about ⅛ inch. Heat the oil to 325–340°F—if you don't have a cooking thermometer, it's about the right temperature when it will brown a small cube of bread in 18 seconds.

Have a plate with a few sheets of paper towel ready by the pan. Depending on the size of your pan, you can probably fry 1–2 pineapple rings at a time.

Using a fork, first dip a pineapple ring into the batter so that it is completely coated, then carefully lower it into the hot oil. After about 1 minute, the side in the oil will have become crisp and brown; use the fork to flip it over. Fry for another 1 minute, then use the fork to lift it out and place it on the paper towels to drain. Let the fritters cool for a few minutes before eating because they will be very hot.

It's easy to create slushy ice treats in exciting flavors and colors —and with a proper deep freeze, you won't have to wait too long for them either. You can use the juices and ready-made smoothie I've mentioned here or choose your own, just make sure they are dairy free and don't contain added sugar.

Stripy Snow Cones

MAKES 4

1⅔ cups pineapple juice
1⅔ cups black grape juice
1 cup strawberry-based dairy-free smoothie
½ cup water

You'll need 3 x 24 oz square or rectangular strong plastic tubs with lids. Pour the pineapple juice into one, the grape juice into the second, and the strawberry smoothie mixed with the measurement water into the third. Place in the deep freeze for 1½ hours.

While the juice freezes, make your cones. Cut 4 circles from foil 10 inches in diameter—draw around a dinner plate or something similar. Cut 2 circles the same size from decorative paper—I like to use wrapping paper, which can be themed if necessary. Cut the wrapping paper circles in half and set aside.

Fold each foil circle in half with the shiny side outermost. Now fold each half into thirds so that you end up with a triangular shape. If you look at the top of the triangle, you'll see that the layers of foil have created a series of triangular pockets. Push your fingers into one pocket and open it out to form a cone. Make sure you can see the matt side of the foil as you look inside the cone—this is vital to ensure you have created a watertight container. Stick a piece of adhesive tape on the seam of the cone to hold everything in place.

Fold each decorative paper semicircle into thirds to create an outer sleeve for each foil cone. Use adhesive tape to secure.

Once your juices and smoothie have had their allotted time in the freezer, bring them out and use a fork to mash into a granular, snowy texture. Lay the cones on their sides and spoon out an even amount of the pineapple ice into each one. Next, add a layer of grape ice. Finally, divide the strawberry smoothie ice between each cone. Serve the cones full of stripy ice immediately, with a straw and teaspoon poked into each one.

Treats & Party Food

Cream, whisky, and a sprinkling of edible gold stars and gold dust make these melt-in-the-mouth truffles extra special. Look for stars or other decorations made without added sugar.

Glittering Chocolate Truffles

MAKES ABOUT 15

3½ oz no-added-sugar semisweet chocolate, broken into small pieces

2 tablespoons unsalted butter, chopped

4 tablespoons light cream

3 teaspoons whisky

scant ¼ cup unsweetened cocoa

1 teaspoon edible gold stars or edible gold dust

Place the chocolate and butter with the cream in a small saucepan over low heat until they have melted, stirring occasionally. Stir in the whisky, then let the mixture cool. Place it in the refrigerator for about 1 hour until it hardens.

Sift the cocoa onto a plate and place a second plate alongside. Scoop out a heaping teaspoonful of the truffle mixture and quickly roll it into a ball in your palms. Place it on the plate with the cocoa and gently shake the plate from side to side until the truffle is well coated, then transfer the truffle to the clean plate. Repeat until all the truffle mixture is used up.

Sprinkle the edible gold stars or some edible gold dust over the truffles to give a touch of magic and sparkle. The truffles will keep in the refrigerator for up to a week.

I find fruity soft-centered chocolates irresistible, so these little hearts tick all the boxes for me. You'll need some small silicone chocolate molds to make them, but these are easily available from cook stores or online.

Apricot Hearts

MAKES ABOUT 18

4 oz no-added-sugar semisweet chocolate, broken into small pieces
scant ¼ cup dried apricots
4 tablespoons water
scant ¼ cup cream cheese
scant ¼ cup ground almonds

Place 3½ oz of the chocolate pieces in a heatproof bowl set over a saucepan of barely simmering water (make sure the bottom of the bowl doesn't touch the water), or in the microwave on a medium setting for about 45 seconds (my preferred method), until nearly all the chocolate has melted. Give it a stir and let rest for a couple of minutes until it has all melted.

Use a teaspoon to smear a layer of melted chocolate around the inside of each mold, making sure the sides and bottoms are well covered. Chill in the refrigerator for about 30 minutes until set.

Meanwhile, finely chop the apricots, place them in a small saucepan with the measurement water, and heat them gently for 5 minutes. Pour the mixture into a mug and add the cream cheese. Insert an immersion blender and blend to create a relatively smooth paste. Stir in the ground almonds. Spoon ½ teaspoonful of apricot filling into each chocolate and use the tip of your finger to smooth it in place so that none of the filling is protruding from the mold. Chill in the refrigerator for another 30 minutes.

Finally, melt the remaining chocolate as before. Use a blunt knife to spread an even layer of melted chocolate over the top of the apricot filling. Chill the chocolates for another 30 minutes until set, then gently pull the silicone apart to release each heart. Turn them out onto a plate and keep chilled until ready to serve. They can be kept for a couple of days in the refrigerator.

Note

Be careful when melting the chocolate—it can be a rather temperamental beast, particularly in situations where you want an attractive finish. The key things to remember are not to let it get too hot and not to allow water into the melted chocolate, otherwise it will "seize" and turn grainy and pastelike. If this happens, you will have to throw it out and start again.

Here I've combined whole-wheat flour and no-added-sugar chocolate to create a healthier version of an enduring favorite—they are always the first to go at a party.

Mini Chocolate Eclairs

MAKES ABOUT 18

For the choux pastry
sunflower oil, for oiling
3½ tablespoons unsalted butter
¾ cup water
generous ¾ cup whole-wheat
    all-purpose flour
2 eggs, beaten

For the topping
3½ oz no-added-sugar milk
    chocolate, broken into small
    pieces
2 tablespoons water

For the filling
1 cup whipping cream

Preheat the oven to 400°F. Lightly oil 2 baking sheets, then run them under cold water in order to wet the surface. Tip the excess water away.

Heat the butter and measurement water in a saucepan until the mixture boils. Take the pan off the heat, add the flour, and quickly whisk everything together (this requires quite a bit of arm strength, so you might want to use an electric whisk). Let the mixture cool for a minute, then whisk in the eggs until you have smooth paste with the consistency of thick custard.

Transfer the paste to a food bag. Snip off the corner, starting your cut about ½ inch along the side of the bag. Pipe out sausage shapes of the paste about 3–3¼ inches long onto the prepared baking sheets, making sure you space them well apart. It can be hard to finish the sausage shapes neatly, though a flick of the wrist usually works well. Use a moistened finger to gently smooth out any lumps that result.

Pop the baking sheets into the oven. After 10 minutes, increase the oven temperature to 425°F and bake the éclairs for another 10 minutes until they are golden brown. Make a small hole in the side of each one with a skewer to release the steam, then let them cool on a wire rack.

Meanwhile, for the topping, place the chocolate and the measurement water in a small saucepan over low heat until the chocolate has melted, stirring occasionally. Pour into a bowl and place in the refrigerator for 15 minutes until it has the consistency of buttercream.

Smooth a layer of the chocolate topping across each éclair and then chill in the refrigerator for 30 minutes until set.

Just before serving, whip the cream until it forms stiff peaks. Cut each éclair in half lengthwise and use a blunt knife to spread a generous quantity of the cream inside, or use a food bag to pipe it in.

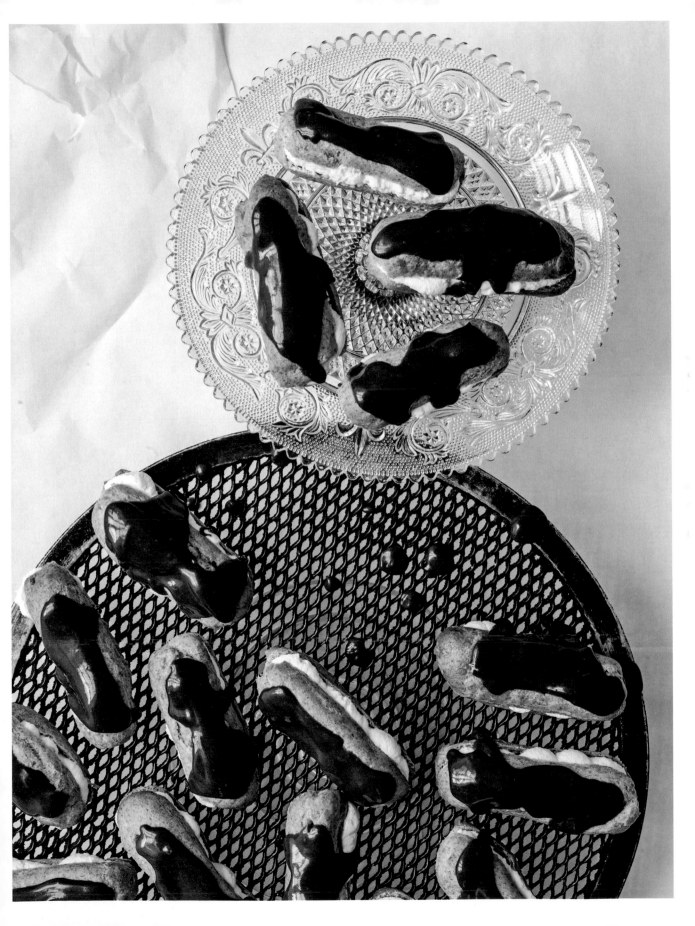

Perfect for those times when you want a treat without too much preparation, this rocky road uses whole-wheat savory crackers alongside fruit and nuts to create a tempting combination of crunch and chew. Finding whole-wheat crackers with no added sugar can be difficult—if you struggle, consider using rough unsweetened oatcakes instead.

Rocky Road

MAKES 16 PIECES

sunflower oil, for oiling
½ cup soft dried apricots
½ cup whole almonds
½ cup whole hazelnuts
2 oz whole-wheat savory crackers
½ cup seedless raisins
5 oz no-added-sugar milk chocolate

Lightly oil an 8 inch square baking pan with a little sunflower oil.

Coarsely chop the dried apricots and nuts. Break the crackers into pieces about ½–1 inch square. Place everything in a bowl and add the raisins.

Break the chocolate into small pieces. Place in a heatproof bowl set over a saucepan of barely simmering water (make sure the bottom of the bowl doesn't touch the water), or in the microwave on a medium setting for about 45 seconds (my preferred method), until nearly all the chocolate has melted. Give it a stir and let rest for a couple of minutes until it has all melted.

Pour the melted chocolate into the bowl with the nut mixture and stir everything well together.

Transfer the mixture to the baking pan and spread it evenly until the pan has been filled. Use a spatula to smooth the surface as much as possible. Chill in the refrigerator for at least an hour until set. Cut into 16 pieces with a sharp knife. You can store the rocky road in an airtight container in the refrigerator for up to a week.

If you're a fan of caramels, you'll be very happy with these chewy chocolate treats. I've specified semisweet chocolate because in the stevia-sweetened brand I use there are far fewer naturally occurring sugars than the milk chocolate version, but it's up to you—these are amazing either way.

Macadamia Chews

MAKES ABOUT 16

½ cup whole macadamia nuts
4 oz chewy dried banana slices
2 teaspoons water
3 oz no-added-sugar semisweet chocolate

Variation

If you use chocolate that is dairy free, this recipe is also suitable for vegans.

Line a baking sheet with silicone parchment paper.

Finely chop one macadamia nut and set aside. Using a large sharp knife, finely chop the banana slices. Place them in a food processor with the remaining nuts and measurement water. Pulse the mixture until the nuts are finely chopped and the mixture is starting to clump together. Give everything a good stir.

Take a heaping teaspoonful of the mixture and roll it firmly into a ball (if the mixture seems crumbly, add a drop more water). Place the ball on a large plate. Repeat until all the mixture has been used up.

Break the chocolate into small pieces. Place in a heatproof bowl set over a saucepan of barely simmering water (make sure the bottom of the bowl doesn't touch the water), or in the microwave on a medium setting for about 45 seconds (my preferred method), until nearly all the chocolate has melted. Give it a stir and let rest for a couple of minutes until it has all melted.

Using 2 forks, roll each ball in the melted chocolate until coated all over. Let the excess chocolate drain through the tines of the forks, then place the ball on the lined baking sheet.

Once all the balls have been coated, sprinkle them with the reserved chopped macadamia nut and then place the baking sheet in the refrigerator until the chocolate has set. The chews should be kept in a cool place and eaten within a week.

This is a simple dessert that nonetheless offers a wealth of possibilities, making it perfect as a party treat or for children. I love serving everyone their fondue in a tea cup, with the assorted items for dipping, impaled on toothpicks, around the saucer. The question is what to dip? You could go for the usual suspects like sliced banana, sliced pineapple, or strawberries, but don't discount the savory options: salted pretzels, crispy bacon, and pitted black olives are all surprisingly delicious too.

Chocolate Fondue

SERVES 6

For the fondue
5 oz no-added-sugar milk chocolate, broken into small pieces
1⅔ cups light cream
3 teaspoons cornstarch
2 tablespoons water

To serve
selection of bite-size food morsels, such as chopped fruit, berries, and savory crackers, for dipping

Place the chocolate with the cream in a small saucepan over low heat until the chocolate has melted, stirring occasionally.

Mix the cornstarch with the measurement water in a cup until smooth. Pour the mixture into the chocolate cream and stir to ensure everything has combined.

Gradually bring the mixture to a boil, stirring continuously, until it has the consistency of custard. Pour your fondue into 6 tea cups and serve immediately, surrounded by your selection of items for dipping.

Baklava is usually steeped in a sugar syrup, but for this version I've used date puree with a hint of lemon. This provides not only sweetness but also nutrients and fiber. The overall effect is gorgeously buttery and nutty, with hints of toffee flavor. This recipe assumes a phyllo pastry sheet size of 12 x 16 inches.

Baklava

MAKES 12

2 oz pitted dried dates, chopped

1 cup water

2 teaspoons fresh lemon juice

1 cup finely chopped raw cashew nuts

½ cup finely chopped shelled raw pistachios

¼ teaspoon ground mixed spice

5 sheets of ready-made phyllo pastry, about 3½ oz total weight

5 tablespoons salted butter, melted

Preheat the oven to 400°F. Line a 12-section muffin pan with paper muffin liners.

Place the dates and measurement water in a blender and blend to a puree. Transfer the puree to a saucepan and bring it to a boil. Reduce the heat to medium and simmer for 15 minutes until the mixture has thickened to the consistency of yogurt, then add the lemon juice. Stir the cashews and pistachios into the date mixture with the mixed spice.

Place the stack of phyllo pastry sheets lengthwise. Now liberally brush melted butter onto the top of each pastry sheet. I find it easiest to do it like this: fold the right-hand side of the top sheet over the left-hand side, almost as if you were turning the pages of a book. Brush melted butter on the exposed surface of the next sheet in the stack, then turn the page, as it were, to expose the next sheet and brush that one with butter too. Continue until you reach the final sheet, then turn all the "pages" back until your sheets are unfolded. Repeat for the left-hand side of each sheet. The final step is to butter the top sheet.

Cut the stack of pastry into 12 squares 4 inches in size. Bring the corners of one square together to form a sort of flower shape and place it in a muffin liner, then repeat for the remaining squares. Pour any remaining melted butter into the date and nut mixture and give it a stir. Place about 3 teaspoonfuls in the center of each liner until all the mixture is used up.

Bake for 20–25 minutes until the pastry has turned golden. These are best served warm, glistening, and crispy from the oven.

Mint and semisweet chocolate are one of those fail-safe combinations. The crunch comes from oatcakes—it doesn't matter if you use the "smooth" or "rough" kind, just as long as they have no added sugar. I've used lucuma powder (see page 186), to add sweetness and because it's packed with nutrients, but if you prefer, you could just add 4 extra dried dates instead.

Mint Chocolate Crunch

MAKES 16 SLICES

7 oz unsweetened oatcakes

3½ oz pitted dried dates

scant ½ cup unsweetened smooth cashew nut butter

1 tablespoon raw lucuma powder (see page 186)

4 teaspoons unsweetened cocoa

2 teaspoons mint extract

7 tablespoons unsalted butter, melted

3½ oz no-added-sugar semisweet chocolate

Variations

If your chocolate is dairy free and you use a dairy-free margarine in place of the butter, this recipe would be suitable for dairy-free and vegan diets. Use gluten-free oatcakes for a gluten-free version of this recipe.

Place the oatcakes, dates, cashew nut butter, lucuma powder, cocoa, and mint extract in a food processor. Pulse until you have a coarse, rubbly mixture.

Pour in the melted butter and stir until everything is well coated. Spoon the mixture into an 8 inch square baking pan and spread it out evenly. Press it down firmly with the back of a metal tablespoon to compact it and flatten the surface.

Break the chocolate into small pieces. Place in a heatproof bowl set over a saucepan of barely simmering water (make sure the bottom of the bowl doesn't touch the water), or in the microwave on a medium setting for about 45 seconds (my preferred method), until nearly all the chocolate has melted. Give it a stir and let rest for a couple of minutes until it has all melted.

Spread the melted chocolate evenly across the minty cookie base with a spatula. Chill in the refrigerator for at least an hour, and then use a sharp knife to cut it into 16 pieces. Keep in the refrigerator until ready to serve. This will keep for up to 3 days.

These simple snacks are great by themselves, or try them dipped into cream cheese or hot chocolate! All you need is a part-baked demi-baguette—one of those bake-at-home breads sold in convenience stores—and a few bits from the pantry. White baguettes are fine, but if you can find a whole-wheat version, so much the better.

Cinnamon Toasts

MAKES ABOUT 40

1 part-baked demi-baguette, about 5 oz
2 tablespoons sunflower oil
2 teaspoons ground cinnamon
1 teaspoon stevia powder (see page 187)

Preheat the oven to 400°F.

Slice the baguette into slices about ¼ inch thick. Brush each side with a little sunflower oil and place on a baking sheet.

Stir the cinnamon and stevia powder together. Sprinkle liberally all across the baguette slices, then shake the baking sheet to get some of the cinnamon mixture on the underside of the slices as well.

Bake for 15 minutes until the baguette slices have become completely hard. Let them cool on a wire rack. Store them in an airtight tin and eat within a week.

Watching a movie just isn't the same without a bowl of popcorn, so if you'd like an alternative to your usual sweet flavor, try this version. The toffee taste of lucuma powder mixed with butter makes for a moreish treat.

Toffee-Flavored Popcorn

SERVES 3–4

1 tablespoon sunflower oil
scant ½ cup popping corn
3½ tablespoons salted butter
4 tablespoons raw lucuma powder
   (see page 186)
2 teaspoons stevia powder
   (see page 187)

Place the oil and popcorn in a 7 inch diameter saucepan and put the lid on. Heat over medium heat. After about 10 minutes you'll hear the corn kernels start to pop; after about 15 minutes they should all be done. Transfer the corn to a large bowl, discarding any unpopped kernels.

Melt the butter in the saucepan that held the corn, then stir in the lucuma powder and stevia powder until combined. Pour the buttery mixture over the corn and toss the corn to get an even coating, then serve.

This is one of those very simple yet stunningly effective recipes. I love how the juicy sweet and fragrant litchis get a hit from the very finely chopped chile, while the cream cheese prevents the combination becoming too fiery. Because chiles vary in their spiciness, choose your quantity according to how much fire you want in your final dish.

Sweet Chile Bites

MAKES ABOUT 15

2–3 red chiles
⅔ cup cream cheese
6 oz pitted fresh or drained
  canned litchis
1 teaspoon paprika

Start by preparing the chiles. Cut the chiles in half lengthwise and remove the pith and seeds, then chop the flesh extremely finely. Stir it into the cream cheese.

Use the handle of a teaspoon to fill each litchi with the cream cheese mixture. Sprinkle the finished bites with the paprika and serve.

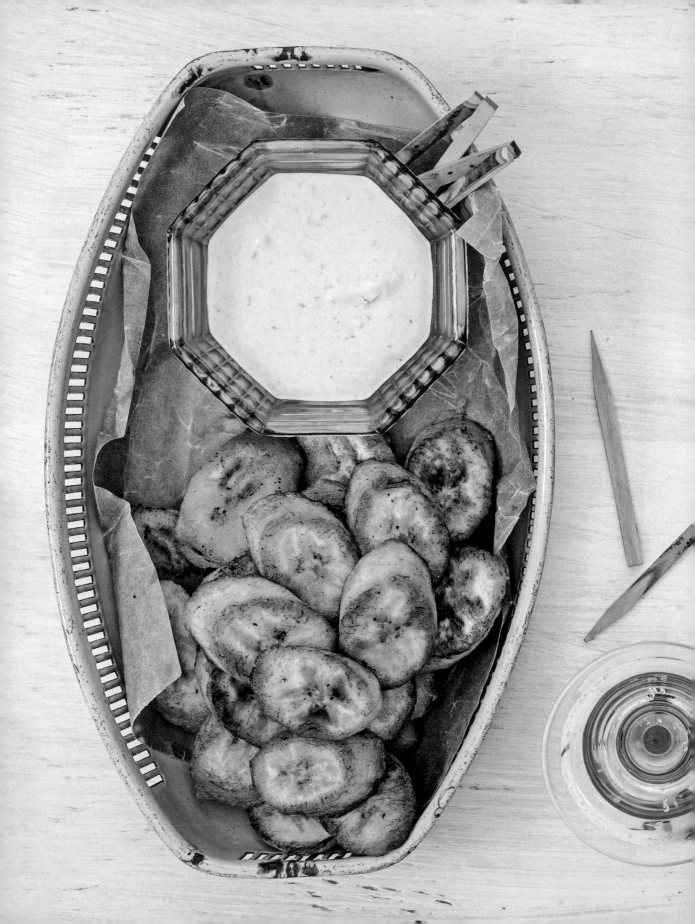

I absolutely adore plantains, especially when they are fried in butter—add a cool smoked chili dip and you have a great party snack. Make sure your plantains have turned black before you use them, though, and don't forget the toothpicks!

Butter-Fried Plantains with Smoky Dip

SERVES 4

4 tablespoons crème fraîche
grated rind of 1 unwaxed lime
 and ½ teaspoon juice
½ teaspoon chipotle paste
3 ripe plantains, about 1 lb 2 oz
 total weight
2 tablespoons salted butter

To make the dip, place the crème fraîche in a serving bowl, then stir in the lime rind and juice and the chipotle paste (use only ¼ teaspoon of the paste if you prefer just a hint of heat).

Trim the plantains, then lightly run a knife down each one to split the skin. Remove the skin and slice the plantains on a slant into pieces roughly ½ inch thick.

Heat the butter in a skillet and fry the plantains over medium-high heat for about 1–2 minutes per side until browned. Serve them as soon as they are done, with the dip alongside.

Sauces, Spreads & Other Basics

The natural sweetness of rice milk is combined with spices to create this ultrasmooth, rich chocolate drink. The topping of whipped cream and chopped pistachios makes it utterly indulgent.

Velvet Hot Chocolate

SERVES 2

¾ cup whipping cream
1 teaspoon cornstarch
3 cups rice milk
2 green cardamom pods
½ teaspoon ground cinnamon, plus extra for serving
6 teaspoons unsweetened cocoa
1 teaspoon chopped unsalted pistachios

Whip the cream until it forms firm peaks and set aside.

Mix the cornstarch with a couple of tablespoons of the rice milk in a cup until smooth. Break the cardamom pods open and remove the seeds. Crush them with the back of a teaspoon.

Place the crushed cardamom seeds in a saucepan with the cinnamon and cocoa over medium heat. Add the remaining rice milk and stir in the cornstarch mixture. Continue stirring until the mixture boils and thickens to a consistency similar to cows' milk. Divide between 2 tall heatproof glasses or mugs.

Spoon or pipe the whipped cream on top of the hot chocolate and sprinkle with the chopped pistachios and a dusting of cinnamon. Serve immediately.

Variation

Served without the cream, this hot chocolate is also suitable for vegan/dairy-free diets.

Thanks to the ground almonds, this buttery, crisp dessert dough has fewer carbohydrates than regular dough, plus more nutrients and fiber. It is also very quick to make!

Low-Carb Dessert Dough

MAKES ABOUT 9 OZ

generous ¾ cup all-purpose flour
½ cup ground almonds
5 tablespoons unsalted butter,
  chilled and cut into chunks
1 egg, beaten

Place the flour, ground almonds, and butter in a food processor. Pulse until you have a mixture with the texture of coffee grounds.

Pour the egg into the flour mixture and then pulse until all the ingredients come together as a yellow dough. Remove the dough from the food processor. It is now ready for use as directed in your recipe.

If you want to make a pastry shell only (blind baking), preheat the oven to 400°F. Roll out the dough on a counter well dusted with flour to a thickness of about ⅛ inch and then cut it a little larger than the intended pan. Press the dough into the pan and trim the excess with a sharp knife. Add a layer of foil, then pour in dried beans or pie weights to fill the pastry shell. Bake for 20 minutes until crisp and just turning golden brown.

Dried milk makes a winning substitute for confectioners' sugar when it comes to frosting. I've formulated 4 common flavors that should give options for every occasion.

Whipped Cake Frosting

MAKES ENOUGH FOR 12 CUPCAKES OR 1 LARGE CAKE

For the basic frosting
2¼ sticks unsalted butter,
  very soft, cut into chunks
scant 1 cup dried milk powder
4 teaspoons stevia powder
  (see page 187)
pinch of salt
2 teaspoons water

For vanilla frosting
2 teaspoons unsweetened vanilla
  extract

For chocolate frosting
¼ cup unsweetened cocoa
2 tablespoons raw lucuma powder
  (see page 186)

For coffee frosting
1 tablespoon raw lucuma powder
  (see page 186)
1 teaspoon unsweetened vanilla
  extract
2 teaspoons instant coffee granules
1 tablespoon boiling water

For zesty frosting
3 tablespoons fresh lemon juice
3 teaspoons grated lime rind

Place the butter in a large bowl. Sift in the milk powder, crushing any larger granules with the back of a teaspoon until it has all passed through the strainer. Whisk everything together thoroughly using an electric whisk. Stir the stevia powder and salt into the measurement water in a cup until dissolved. Whisk into the butter mixture until you have a pale mixture with a light texture. The frosting is now ready to be flavored from the choices below.

For vanilla frosting, whisk the frosting and vanilla extract together until thoroughly combined. The frosting is now ready to use.

For chocolate frosting, sift the cocoa and lucuma powder into the frosting and whisk together to create a smooth, rich paste ready to frost your cake.

For coffee frosting, add the lucuma powder and vanilla extract to the frosting. Dissolve the coffee granules in the measurement boiling water and pour into the frosting. Whisk everything together until thoroughly combined. The frosting is now ready to use.

For zesty frosting, whisk the lemon juice into the frosting, then stir in the lime rind. The frosting is now ready to use.

Note
Keep frosted cakes in the refrigerator until needed and eat the frosting within 48 hours.

Use this silky white sauce cold as a low-fat alternative to cream, or hot instead of regular vanilla custard. Rice milk gives a wonderful natural sweetness, while the vanilla bean adds a touch of luxury.

Vanilla Cream

MAKES ABOUT 2 CUPS

scant 1½ cups rice milk
1 vanilla bean
2 tablespoons cornstarch
½ teaspoon stevia powder
(see page 187)
¾ cup light cream

Pour the rice milk into a small saucepan. Carefully cut down the length of the vanilla bean and scrape out the seeds into the rice milk, then add the empty bean as well. Bring to a boil, then remove the bean.

Mix the cornstarch and stevia powder with the cream in a bowl until smooth. Whisk into the hot rice milk and bring to a boil, whisking continously. The mixture will thicken to the consistency of Greek yogurt.

Remove from the heat and pour it into a pitcher. You can either serve it immediately, or let it cool completely before giving it another quick stir and serving it cold.

This buttery orange sauce is just perfect for pancakes—or if you are feeling really indulgent, you could use it on my Vanilla Ice Cream (see page 89) in place of syrupy toppings. If you want to maximize your nutrients, use 4 large, freshly squeezed oranges instead of juice from a carton.

Orange Dessert Sauce

MAKES ABOUT 1¼ CUPS

generous 2 cups fresh orange juice
   with bits
7 tablespoons unsalted butter,
   chopped
1 teaspoon cornstarch
½ teaspoon stevia powder
   (see page 187)

Set 2 tablespoons of the orange juice aside, then heat the rest in a saucepan until it boils. Add the butter and stir until it has melted. Let the mixture boil for 10 minutes until it has reduced by about one-third.

Mix the cornstarch and stevia powder into the reserved orange juice in a bowl until smooth. Whisk into the hot boiling butter/juice mixture and bring to a boil, whisking continuously. The mixture will thicken to the consistency of thick cream.

Remove the sauce from the heat and use immediately.

Coulis is a fancy name for a dessert sauce and most standard recipes contain added sugar. This mango version uses just fresh fruit and takes only moments to make. Try it poured over my Fresh Fig Panna Cotta (see page 82), drizzled over a cream cake, or even served alongside roast chicken.

Mango Coulis

MAKES ABOUT ⅔ CUP

1 medium ripe mango (about 10 oz), peeled and seed removed
2 tablespoons fresh orange juice with bits, plus extra if needed

Place the mango flesh and orange juice in a blender and blend until smooth.

Rub the mixture through a strainer to leave a smooth puree with the consistency of yogurt. It should be quite easy to pour. If the coulis seems too thick, add a drop more orange juice. This is best used the same day.

A compote of mixed berries is an easy way to boost your fruit intake: try it on oatmeal, with pancakes, or simply topped with a little plain yogurt. This recipe works well with fresh or frozen berries.

Mixed Berry Compote

SERVES 3–4

1⅓ cups fresh or frozen mixed raspberries, blackberries, and black currants
1 banana, about 5 oz

Place the berries in a saucepan. Peel and mash the banana, then add to the pan over medium-low heat. Place the lid on the pan and cook for 10–15 minutes, stirring occasionally. The compote is done when the banana seems to have disappeared and you are left with a juicy mixture but with most of the berries still reasonably intact.

You can serve the compote warm or cold. It will keep for up to 3 days in the refrigerator.

Variation

You can use other types of berries for this compote, as long as there are always some naturally sweeter ones like strawberries, raspberries, or blueberries alongside the more sour varieties such as black currants or gooseberries.

This tangy orange and apricot curd is perfect for spreading on English muffins, toast, or scones, and also makes a delicious filling and/or topping for a cake.

Orange & Apricot Curd

MAKES ABOUT 1 CUP

generous ½ cup dried apricots
½ cup water
grated rind of 1 small unwaxed
    orange and 3 tablespoons juice
1 egg
3½ tablespoons unsalted butter,
    chopped
pinch of salt

Soak the apricots in the measurement water for 4 hours or overnight.

Place the apricots in a blender, add the orange rind and juice, and egg. Blend the mixture until smooth.

Transfer the apricot mixture to a small saucepan with the butter and salt. Heat gently until the butter melts, stirring continuously. Continue cooking for about 5–10 minutes until the mixture has become so thick that you can't see the bottom of the pan as you stir.

Remove the pan from the heat and let the curd cool completely before transferring it to an airtight jar. It will keep for up to a week in the refrigerator.

Jams were originally invented as a way to preserve fruit out of season—and just also happened to be delicious on toast. However, what with modern refrigeration and year-round fresh fruit, drowning strawberries in sugar is not essential anymore. But if you still want something for toast, here's how.

Strawberry Jam

MAKES ABOUT 1 CUP

1 dessert apple, about 6 oz, cored and coarsely shredded (leave the skin on)

generous 1⅓ cups fresh strawberries, hulled and coarsely chopped

2 teaspoons stevia powder (see page 187)

½ teaspoon fresh lemon juice

Place all the ingredients in a saucepan with a tight-fitting lid and cook over medium heat for 20 minutes, stirring occasionally. At the end of this time, the apple will have lost most of its structure and the strawberries will have spread their red juices throughout the mix.

Take the lid off the pan, turn the heat up a notch, and let the jam bubble gently for 5 minutes or so until it thickens. Let cool.

You can either store the jam in airtight jar in the refrigerator for up to a week or, if you prefer handy portions that will last longer than this, divide the jam between the sections of an ice cube tray, then cover with foil and freeze. That way, you can defrost it as and when necessary.

Standard chocolate hazelnut spreads are loaded with sugar, but making your own is surprisingly quick and easy to do. This recipe provides a reasonably small amount, but it's best to make it little and often because there is no sugar to act as a preservative.

Chocolate Hazelnut Spread

MAKES ABOUT ½ CUP

scant ¼ cup raw hazelnuts, coarsely chopped
4 tablespoons sunflower oil
¼ cup dried milk powder
1 tablespoon unsweetened cocoa
2 teaspoons stevia powder (see page 187)
4 tablespoons boiling water

Toast the chopped hazelnuts in a dry skillet over medium-high heat for 3–4 minutes, stirring occasionally, until they have turned golden brown.

Place the nuts with the oil, milk powder, and cocoa in a bowl. Use an immersion blender to blend everything together until you have a dark, oily, and somewhat grainy mixture. This will take up to a minute.

Stir the stevia powder into the measurement boiling water in a cup until dissolved. While continuing to blend, slowly pour the stevia mixture into the nut mixture. Suddenly everything will combine into a smooth paste. Transfer it to a small airtight jar and refrigerate. Once it has chilled it will have the consistency of soft butter.

The spread will keep in the refrigerator for up to 3 days. It also freezes well —just allow it to defrost and give it a stir before use.

Chutneys and pickles are relatively sugary foods, so if you want to cut back on sugar, it makes sense to reduce the amount you consume in this way. My quick pickle won't keep for longer than a few days and is sweetened only with apple, but it still makes a tasty accompaniment to cold meats and cheeses.

Quick Apple Pickle

MAKES ABOUT 1 CUP

1 teaspoon sunflower oil
1 small dessert apple, peeled, cored, and finely chopped
½ small onion, finely chopped
4 tablespoons apple puree
1 tablespoon golden raisins
1 teaspoon cider vinegar
1 teaspoon whole-grain mustard
½ teaspoon ground ginger
½ teaspoon ground coriander
pinch of salt

Heat the oil in a saucepan and fry the apple and onion over medium-high heat for 3–4 minutes until the apple has softened and the onion has become slightly translucent.

Remove from the heat and stir in all the remaining ingredients. Let cool, then store in an airtight jar in the refrigerator for up to 3 days.

This homemade sauce makes a good alternative to ready-made sweet chili sauces, which often have added sugar. It has a piquant sweet-and-sour flavor that is great as an accompaniment to egg rolls, dumplings, or sushi.

Asian-Style Dipping Sauce

MAKES ABOUT ⅓ CUP

4 tablespoons good-quality fresh apple juice
1 tablespoon light soy sauce
½ teaspoon garlic puree
¼ teaspoon ground ginger
1 teaspoon rice wine vinegar or cider vinegar
¼ hot red chile, seeded and thinly sliced
1 teaspoon finely chopped chives

Stir the apple juice and soy sauce together in a small serving bowl. Mix the garlic puree and ginger into the vinegar in a cup until smooth, then stir into the apple juice/soy mixture.

Add the chile and chives, then serve.

Variation

Make this sauce gluten free by using gluten-free tamari in place of the soy sauce.

Ketchup is around 25 percent sugar—it's practically jam!
—which is why, of course, it tastes so good. The sugar and
vinegar are designed to preserve it, but it's easy to make
a quick version in small batches and keep it in the refrigerator.
There is still sweetness here, but it comes only from the fruits
and is accompanied by their nutrients as well.

Tomato Ketchup

MAKES ABOUT ¼ CUP

2 tablespoons apple puree
1 tablespoon tomato paste
1 teaspoon cider vinegar
½ teaspoon garlic puree
pinch of ground black pepper
pinch of ground allspice

Place all the ingredients in a bowl and stir well. The ketchup is now ready
to serve, but if you don't want to use it all at once, transfer to an airtight
container and place in the refrigerator—it will keep for up to a week.

There are many, many uses for this creamy egg-free mayo—
it's great in a chicken sandwich, supertasty smothered on new
potatoes, and perfect as a dip. I love it because it's easy to make
and full of avocado goodness, without any added sweeteners.

Avocado Mayonnaise

MAKES ABOUT ⅔ CUP

5oz avocado flesh (about
   1 avocado)
generous ⅓ cup olive oil
1 tablespoon cornstarch
2 tablespoons fresh lemon juice
1½ teaspoons garlic puree

Place all the ingredients in a blender and blend until thick and completely
smooth—about 2 minutes or so. Let sit for a couple of minutes. Now
blend again for another minute. This method helps the mayonnaise to
stay creamy and prevent it from separating.

....

Serve immediately or scrape everything into an airtight container and
refrigerate until needed. Give it a quick stir before serving. It will keep
for up to 3 days without going brown.

Many prepared salad dressings contain hidden sugar, so making your own is a good way to eliminate unnecessary carbs from your diet. This recipe will give you a good basic vinaigrette. You can then play around with the formula by using different kinds of oil or vinegar, or by adding other flavorings such as chopped herbs or mustard powder.

Vinaigrette Dressing

MAKES ABOUT ⅓ CUP

4 tablespoons olive oil
1 tablespoon white wine vinegar
1 teaspoon garlic puree
large pinch of ground black pepper

Place all the ingredients in a pot with a lid, then shake thoroughly before drizzling over your salad. The dressing will keep for a couple of weeks in the refrigerator.

Variation

You can make a creamy dressing by adding 2 tablespoons crumbled feta cheese or blue cheese and 1 tablespoon light cream to the dressing and whisking everything together thoroughly before use. The dressing will keep for a couple of days in the refrigerator.

Glossary

The following is a guide to some of the sweeteners and more unusual ingredients that I use in my recipes.

Agar powder

Agar (or agar-agar) powder is a natural gelling agent that comes from freeze-dried seaweed. Suitable for vegetarians and vegans, it helps to prevent the growth of ice crystals in frozen foods and give a satiny mouthfeel to ice cream. It is sometimes sold as flakes. If you can't find agar powder, carrageenan powder (made from another kind of seaweed) can be used instead.

Almond milk

This dairy-free alternative to cows' milk is made from a filtered blend of almonds and water, and provides an assortment of nutrients. Make sure the product you choose is unsweetened; it is naturally sugar free. You can use soy milk instead if you prefer.

Apple puree

I use apple puree to sweeten some of my dishes. It can be tricky to find, but the baby food aisle of the grocery store is a good place to source it, especially if only a small amount is needed. If you want to make your own, finely chop a peeled, cored cooking apple and heat gently in a saucepan with 2 tablespoons apple juice until the apple has become pulpy. Let cool before use.

Chestnut flour

Made from ground dried chestnuts, chestnut flour is naturally gluten free. High in fiber and very nutritious, it also has a natural sugar content of about 20 percent, which means that chestnut flour can be used as a wheat flour substitute in cakes with few, if any, further sweeteners needed.

Evaporated milk

This is milk that has been boiled for a long time until it becomes thick and gloopy, a process that concentrates its natural sugar (lactose) content. It can be useful in some recipes, though it has a distinctive taste. It usually comes in a can. Evaporated milk is not to be confused with condensed milk, which has added sugar.

Honey

Chemically speaking, honey is not much different to diluted table sugar, though good-quality honey also contains a mixture of minerals and other nutrients. I use it very sparingly and always choose a raw local organic honey.

No-added-sugar chocolate

As distinct from unsweetened chocolate (which is rather bitter), no-added-sugar chocolate is still somewhat sweet but is sweetened without sugar. It is sometimes marketed as diabetic chocolate. The brand I use contains stevia, but look out for others sweetened with erythritol or maltitol, which are low-calorie naturally derived sweeteners. If you can't find them in your grocery store, try health food stores or online suppliers. Normally both semisweet and milk versions are available. This kind of chocolate is useful for adding a touch of luxury to desserts and cake, but bear in mind that it is still high in calories.

Raw lucuma powder

This low-GI sweetener comes from a nutritious South American fruit with a very hard flesh, which is ground up into a powder that has a malty toffee–date flavor. It is useful in some recipes, but the drawback is that the powder doesn't dissolve, so it's not suitable as a sugar alternative for sprinkling on doughnuts or cereal, for instance, because it will just taste "claggy."

Rice milk

Made from blended rice, water, and oil, rice milk should not contain any added sweeteners. Although the total sugar content is the same as cows' milk (about 4 percent), it tastes sweeter. This is useful in recipes because it means that the need for further sweetening is reduced.

Stevia powder

I use the term "stevia powder" in my recipes to refer to sweeteners based on stevia extracts. There are many such products on the market and the precise extract of the stevia plant used varies, as does the added ingredients. I like stevia because it is naturally derived and only a little is needed. I keep the amounts of stevia I use to a minimum—just enough to make the recipes pleasantly sweet, but without the aftertaste becoming noticeable. The brand I use has added erythritol, a low calorie, naturally derived sweetener, and is about three times sweeter than ordinary white sugar. But don't feel you have to use stevia powder at all—there are many other alternative sweeteners available.

Index

Acknowledgments

To the STARS, may they always shine.

Author's acknowledgments
For support and practical help of many kinds I want to thank Mom and Dad, Richard, Phil, Chris, and Maureen; Hannah Booth, Hannah Johnston, and Jason Taylor at DFC; Allyson Bates; Zoe Bailey; Becky Boyd; Ruth Gillingham; Nina Hertig; Becky and Chris Knapp; Allison Macfarlan; Esther Porta; Lucie Roberts; Helen Rossiter, and Andrea Wood.

Thank you to everyone who tested my recipes, including Anne and Matt Balme, Anna Barrett, Jacky Booth, Tania Fish, Kim and Richard Lankshear, Rose Lewis, Felicia Parker, and Eric Trolle.

Thank you to my agent Eve White and her assistant Jack Ramm for their ideas. At Octopus I am grateful as ever to Stephanie, Alex, Jaz, Abigail, and the rest of the team for such a beautiful book. Thanks too to Kat Mead, Siân Henley, and Liz and Max Haarala Hamilton, who helped to bring the recipes to life and gave me some brilliant memories, especially when it comes to citrus.

About the author
Susanna Booth is a passionate and inventive self-taught chef who specializes in creating recipes for specific dietary requirements. A former recipe columnist for the Guardian, she uses her degree in Polymer Chemistry to offer a fresh perspective on some of our best-loved dishes.

An Hachette UK Company
www.hachette.co.uk
First published in Great Britain in 2016
by Hamlyn, a division of
Octopus Publishing Group Ltd
Carmelite House
50 Victoria Embankment
London EC4Y 0DZ

Distributed in the US by
Hachette Book Group
1290 Avenue of the Americas
4th and 5th Floors
New York, NY 10020

Distributed in Canada by
Canadian Manda Group
664 Annette St.
Toronto, Ontario, Canada M6S 2C8

ISBN 978 0 60063 252 8

A CIP catalogue record for this book is available from the British Library

Printed and bound in China

10 9 8 7 6 5 4 3 2 1

Publishing Director—Stephanie Jackson
Art Director—Jonathan Christie
Design—Jaz Bahra
Senior Editor—Alex Stetter
Copy Editor—Jo Richardson
Ilustrations—Abigail Read
Photography—Haarala Hamilton
Home Economist and Food Stylist—Kat Mead
Nutritionist—Angela Dowden
Production Controller—Meskerem Berhane